Asher Israelowitz's

Guide to Jewish Europe

Western Europe Edition

Library of Congress Catalogue Card Number: 84-090694
International Standard Book Number: 0-9611036-1-2

Printed in the United States of America

Book design by Jane Berger

Cover Photo
Interior of Bevis Marks Synagogue, London

Contents

ix **Introduction**

xi **Touring Tips**

1 **Spain**
3 Barcelona
4 Cordoba
5 Granada
6 Madrid
7 Malaga
8 Mallorca
8 Marbella
9 Segovia
10 Seville
11 Toledo
16 Side Trips
18 Synagogues
19 Mikvehs
19 Kosher Restaurants
19 American Express Offices
20 Youth Hostels
21 Railroad Timetables

22 **Gibraltar**
26 Kosher Restaurants
26 American Express Office

27 **Portugal**
27 Lisbon
28 Porto
28 Tomar
28 Faro
29 Synagogues
29 Kosher Provisions
29 American Express Offices
30 Youth Hostels
30 Railroad Timetables

31 **France**
34 Paris
41 Lunéville
42 Saarebourg
42 Strasbourg
44 Provence
47 Marseille
47 Nice
48 Cannes
48 Monaco-Monte Carlo
49 Synagogues
54 Mikvehs
55 Kosher Restaurants
57 American Express Offices
58 Youth Hostels

59 Railroad Timetables

61 **Italy**
63 Rome
69 Venice
78 Florence
81 Leghorn (Livorno)
82 Turin
86 Synagogues
87 Mikvehs
89 Kosher Hotels
88 Kosher Restaurants
89 American Express Offices
90 Youth Hostels
91 Railroad Timetables

92 **Germany**
94 Ansbach
96 Berlin
99 Cologne
100 Dachau
101 Essen
102 Frankfurt-am-Main
103 Schwäbisch Hall
104 Worms
110 Synagogues
112 Mikveh
113 Kosher Provisions
113 American Express Offices
114 Youth Hostels
115 Railroad Timetables

116 **Switzerland**
118 Endingen-Lengnau
120 Basel
120 Bern
121 Synagogues
122 Mikvehs
123 Kosher Restaurants
124 American Express Offices
125 Youth Hostels
126 Railroad Timetables

127 **Austria**
127 Synagogues
128 Mikvehs
128 Kosher Restaurants
128 American Express Offices
129 Youth Hostels
129 Railroad Timetables

130 **Prague, Czechoslovakia**
139 American Express Offices
139 Youth Hostels

140 **Budapest, Hungary**
142 Synagogue
142 Mikveh
143 Kosher Restaurants
143 American Express Offices
143 Youth Hostels

144 **Belgium**
145 Synagogues
146 Mikvehs
146 Kosher Restaurants
147 American Express Offices
147 Youth Hostels
147 Railroad Timetables

149 **Netherlands**
150 Amsterdam
157 Synagogues
158 Mikvehs
159 Kosher Restaurants

159 American Express Offices
159 Youth Hostels
160 Railroad Timetables

161 **Luxembourg**
161 Synagogues
161 American Express Office
161 Youth Hostel

162 **Denmark**
164 Copenhagen
166 Synagogues
166 Mikvehs
166 Kosher Restaurants
166 American Express Offices
167 Youth Hostels
167 Railroad Timetables

168 **Sweden**
168 Gothenburg
169 Malmö
169 Stockholm
170 Synagogues
170 Mikvehs
170 Kosher Restaurants
171 American Express Offices
171 Youth Hostels
171 Railroad Timetables

172 **Finland**
173 Helsinki
173 Ahvenanmaa Islands
173 Kosher Restaurants
174 American Express Offices
174 Youth Hostels
174 Railroad Timetables

175 **Norway**
175 Oslo
175 Trondheim
176 Kosher Restaurants
176 American Express Offices
177 Youth Hostels
177 Railroad Timetables

178 **Great Britain**
181 Brighton
181 Lincoln
182 London
194 Manchester
195 Glasgow
195 York
197 Synagogues
203 Mikvehs
204 Kosher Restaurants
206 American Express Offices
208 Youth Hostels
209 Railroad Timetables

210 **Ireland**
210 Synagogues
210 Kosher Provisions

211 **Sabbath Candlelighting Timetables**

217 **Israeli Folk Dancing**

218 **Bibliography**

220 **Glossary**

226 **Biography**

227 **Index**

Europe

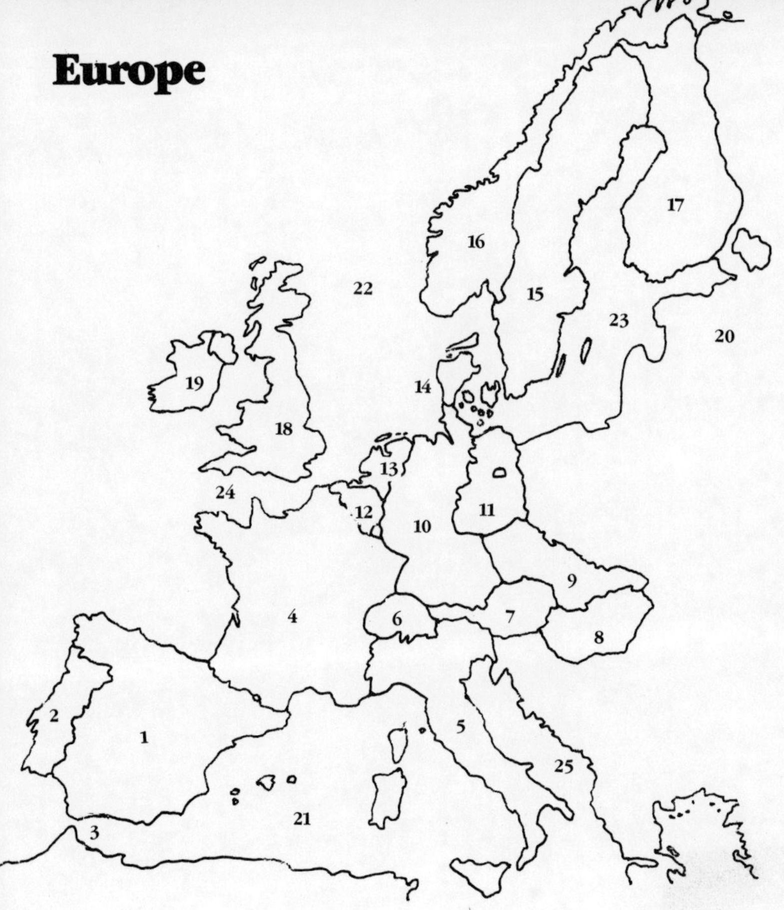

1 Spain
2 Portugal
3 Gibraltar
4 France
5 Italy
6 Switzerland
7 Austria
8 Hungary
9 Czechoslovakia
10 West Germany
11 East Germany
12 Belgium
13 Netherlands
14 Denmark
15 Sweden
16 Norway
17 Finland
18 Great Britain
19 Ireland
20 Soviet Union
21 Mediterranean Sea
22 North Sea
23 Baltic Sea
24 English Channel
25 Adriatic Sea

Introduction

The *Guide to Jewish Europe* is designed to assist the first-time traveler as well as the seasoned-traveler by providing up-to-date information on Jewish life in Europe. The book is divided into five sections or regions: the Sephardic countries (those lands around the Mediterranean Sea), the Ashkenazic countries (those lands of Germanic or Yiddish-speaking Jewish communities), the Benelux countries, Scandinavia, and the British Isles. Each section is further divided into individual countries or cities. For each country or city there is complete information on kosher restaurants, butchers, bakeries, and hotels. There is information on Jewish historic landmarks, museums, synagogues, cemeteries, and mikvehs (mikvaot). There are also lists of American Express offices, youth hostels, intercity railroad schedules, and Sabbath candlelighting timetables. There are many maps as well as many photographs which will assist the traveler in locating his or her destination.

The Guide provides telephone numbers of the local Jewish community centers and synagogues. The contact people in each city, usually the rabbi of the community, will be more than happy to assist the Jewish traveler with regard to kosher eateries, local customs, synagogue services, and special events. The rabbi may not always be conversant in the English language, so the old stand-by languages of Hebrew or Yiddish will come in very handy.

There's so much to see and do in Jewish Europe, so have your airline tickets and passports ready, and let's begin.

Touring Tips

- The most important tip anyone can tell you when traveling is to "travel light."
- Minimize the amount of money or credit cards that you carry with you.
- Carry traveler's checks; they are replaceable if lost or stolen.
- If you are traveling in the summer, bring an extra (heavy) sweater—northern European countries are usually very cool, especially when it rains. It can be very nasty and raw.
- Bring a (fold-up) travel umbrella. It can sometimes rain for several days.
- Buy color photographic film at home. Color film in Europe is very expensive (almost double the price). Black and white film, however, is comparable in price.
- When going through security X-ray machines at airports, remove all of your rolls of film and ask the security agent to "hand-inspect" your film. This will prevent the film from possibly becoming "fogged-up" as it passes through the X-rays. You can also purchase a "lead-coated" camera bag, but you will have to carry that extra weight throughout Europe.
- Change your money into foreign currency before you enter the next European country. When you arrive, you will then have change for buses, trains, taxis, telephones, or meals.

- Most credit cards (Visa, Mastercard, American Express) are accepted in all European countries, including the Eastern Bloc (Communist) lands.
- Don't ever leave your passport or train or airplane ticket unattended. If you will not carry on the Sabbath, you can leave them with your other valuables in your hotel safe.
- Most breads in Europe are not kosher! The pans in which breads are baked are usually smeared with lard or shortening. Hearth-baked breads are permitted to be eaten—if you can ascertain that they were not prepared with shortening. Most French breads are kosher (in France and Italy). Ask the local rabbi which breads are permissible in each city or buy breads in a kosher bakery. Most breads with a glazed surface are not kosher.
- Some vinegars in Italy are made with (non-kosher) wines. Be careful when you are having your vegetable salad at a hotel or restaurant.
- In France, although many of the kosher restaurants are under rabbinical supervision, this supervision applies only to the foods served—it does not always apply to the wines which accompany the meal. Check before you drink!
- In Italy, there have been problems with kosher meats. It is recommended to ascertain if the restaurant is under rabbinical supervision.
- Many European cities have trolley systems which do not have conductors aboard. These trolley systems (e.g. Amsterdam or Zurich) are designed on an honor system. You are required to purchase a ticket before you enter the tram at a machine on the tram station or at the main railroad terminal. If you are caught by an inspector, who might just happen to board your tram car, you will be given a stiff fine if you don't have a ticket, usually about $20.00. So, to avoid much embarrassment and a penalty, get your tram ticket before you board the trolley.

- In the Paris Metro and the London Underground, be sure to hold onto your ticket until after you exit, otherwise you may have to pay a penalty of a full fare. In London, there are station guards who collect your ticket as you exit.
- In the London Underground, you can purchase an all-day pass (for two pounds) which is valid for unlimited bus and subway (tube) travel throughout the city.
- When crossing the street in England, remember to always first look to the right! Traffic patterns are reversed in England.
- When boarding an intercity train, make sure that the car you are in is marked with the proper destination sign of your intended destination. Sometimes long trains are broken into sections; with some cars going to Paris, some going to Marseille, and others going to Geneva.
- In Spanish train stations, there are no luggage-storage areas. This is because of terrorist attacks in train terminals several years ago. When you arrive in a Spanish city, you can leave your baggage near the train terminal, in a local cafe or restaurant.
- The Spanish railroads are few and usually very crowded. You must have a seat reservation on all intercity trains. If you already have a Eurailpass you are still required to get this computerized seat reservation (but at no additional cost).
- When entering a city, deposit your heavy baggage at the luggage-storage area. You are now ready to look for a hotel accommodation. You can approach the local tourist information center, which is usually located in or near the train terminal. Ask for a map of the city and where you might find a room. These people speak English and actually have such a hotel service (for a nominal fee). You can look for a hotel room on your own. The best time of day to do this is around noon, when many hotel guests are checking out. Look for a hotel near the synagogue and/or kosher restaurant.
- Youth hostels offer low-cost accommodation to young people on their travels. They vary greatly from country to country.

Some hostels are in old houses or castles, or modern buildings. They provide separate sleeping accommodation and washing and toilet facilities for men and for women. Accommodation is usually in dormitories (generally bunk beds), sometimes with as few as four beds, sometimes as many as twenty. There are no kosher facilties in these youth hostels. In order to use the youth hostels of any country in Europe, you must have a youth hostel membership card. For further information contact The International Youth Hostel Center at 132 Spring Street, New York, New York 10012 or call (212)431-7100.

NOTE: All timetables in this guide are in *military time*.

- The milk in Spain is not kosher! The heavy cream is removed and is replaced with (animal) fat! There is no government control over milk additives.

IMPORTANT NOTE: Although every effort has been made to ensure accuracy, changes will occur after the "guide" has gone to press. Particular attention must be drawn to the fact that kosher food establishments change hands often and suddenly, in some cases going over to a non-kosher ownership. No responsiblity, therefore, can be taken for the absolute accuracy of the information, and visitors are advised to obtain confirmation of kashruth claims.

Spain

It is said that the Jews first came to Spain, *Sfarad*, after the destruction of the Holy Temple in Jerusalem in 586 B.C.E. The Visigoths, who occupied Spain in the 5th century, embraced Christianity, and persecuted its Jewish and Moslem population. The Moslems (Moors and Berbers), from North Africa, conquered Spain in 711. It was during this Moslem rule that the Jews prospered to such a great degree that the era became known as the "Golden Age of Spain." Under the caliphs, the Jews produced poets, philosophers, scientists, scholars, statesmen, financiers, and royal advisers. The Jewish scholars translated into Hebrew and Latin the classical Greek writings which were written in Arabic. These classical writings would reappear in a new era, the Renaissance. Some eminent Jews in medieval Spain include: Moses Maimonides (Rambam), Yehuda Halevi, Benjamin of Tudela, and Issac Abarbanel.

The Christian rulers drove most of the Moslems from Spain by the beginning of the 13th century. This was known as the *Reconquista*. In 1391, the Christian mobs annihilated the Jewish quarters of Seville, Barcelona, Cordoba, and Toledo. This was the beginning of the end of Jewish settlement in Spain. Jews at this time chose to convert publicly to Christianity and would actually eat pork in the public squares to prove their outward Christianity. However, at home, they would still practice their Jewish faith. These secret Jews were known as *Marranos*, which means "pig" in Spanish. In 1478, the Inquisition, which sought to destroy

SPAIN

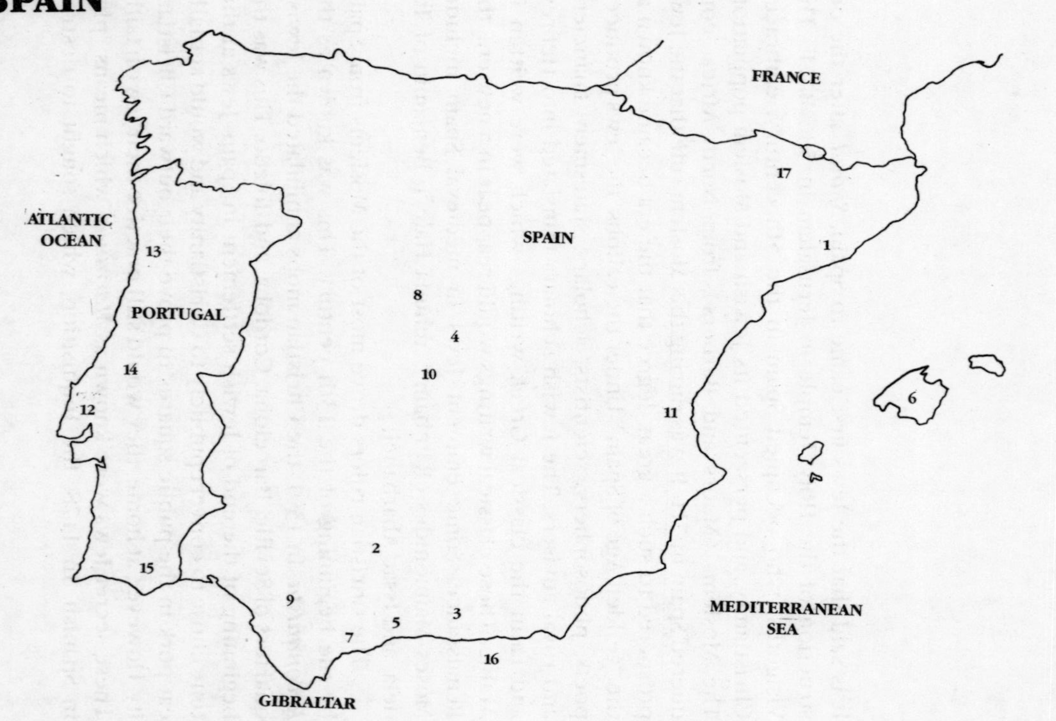

1 Barcelona
2 Cordoba
3 Granada
4 Madrid
5 Malaga
6 Mallorca
7 Marbella
8 Segovia
9 Seville
10 Toledo
11 Valencia
12 Lisbon
13 Porto
14 Tomar
15 Faro
16 Costa del Sol
17 Andorra

these Marranos with every type of weapon, including death by torture, was established. On March 30, 1492, King Ferdinand V and Queen Isabella signed the decree expelling all Jews from Spain. The Jews were given four months, until August 1, 1492 to leave. This was the day of *Tish'a Ba'av*, the fast of the ninth day of the Hebrew month of Av, which commemorates the destruction of the first and second Holy Temples in Jerusalem. The Inquisition was not abolished until 1868. Sephardic Jews from North Africa and Greece were the first Jews to resettle in Spain. During the 1930s and 1940s, Francisco Franco, admitted as many as 40,000 Jews from Nazi-occupied territories in Europe. It has been said that Franco was descended from Marranos. There are about 12,000 Jews living in Spain today. The largest Jewish communities are in Madrid and Barcelona.

BARCELONA

Spain's second largest city, Barcelona has a Jewish population of over 5,000. The first synagogue building on Spanish soil since the expulsion of 1492, was erected in 1954. The synagogue houses a Sephardic congregation on the first floor and an Ashkenazic congregation on the third floor. The building located at *24 Calle Porvenir* also houses a Jewish Community Center.

CARRER DELL CALL

A street located in the oldest section of the city, was once the Juderia, the Jewish quarter. In Catalan, the word "Call" means "kahal" or congregation or synagogue.

MONTJUICH

Barcelona is cradled between two hills, Tibidabo and Montjuich. Montjuich is the Catalan word for "Mountain of the Jews." In the 11th and 12th centuries, many Jews owned land on the slopes of this mountain. Here too was a Jewish cemetery which was abandoned after the massacres of 1391. Some of the tombstones from this cemetery are on display in a special room in the Historical Museum of Barcelona in the city's Old Gothic quarter.

CORDOBA

ALMODOVAR GATE

This was the entrance into the old Jewish quarter. It was known as the *Bab-al-Yahud*, 'Gate of the Jews.'

CALLE JUDA LEVI

This street was named for Judah Halevi, the medieval poet who was born in Toledo in 1075 but lived most of his life in Cordoba.

RAMBAM (MAIMONIDES) STATUE

Moshe ben Maimon was born in Cordoba in 1135. At the age of 13, Maimonides and his family fled the city when the Almohades, fanatical Berber tribesmen from North Africa, crossed the Straits of Gibraltar and conquered Cordoba. Maimonides became the noted theologian, philosopher, and physician. His monumental works, the *Mishneh Torah* and *The Guide to the Perplexed*, were written in North Africa. His sojourns include Fez, Morocco, Alexandria and Cairo, Egypt and, finally, to his resting place in Tiberias, Israel. The Maimonides statue was erected by the Spanish government in 1964.

RAMBAM SYNAGOGUE 20 Calle de los Judios

A small moorish building built in 1315 is now a national monument. From the women's gallery, one can see the handsomely carved plasterwork above the niche where the holy ark stood and where the Torah scrolls were kept. A Hebrew inscription on the wall establishes the name of the founder or donor, Isaac Moheb. After the expulsion of the Jews in 1492, the synagogue was converted into a quarantine hospital for victims of rabies, an oratory for the guild of shoemakers and, centuries later, was converted into the Church of St. Crispin. The building was partially restored in 1935 as a synagogue in commemoration of the 800th anniversary of the birth of Maimonides.

GRANADA

The 10th century Arab historians called this city *Gharnatat al-Yahud*, 'Granada of the Jews.' It has been said, "Whoever has not seen the splendor of the Jews of Granada, their fortune and their glory, has never seen true glory." This description applies most aptly to Shmuel ha-Nagid (993-1055), who was a field commander of the army, Talmud scholar,Hebrew poet, mathematician, and philosopher. His son, Joseph ibn-Naghdela, built the oldest sections of the Alhambra, Spain's most beautiful palace and fortress.

ALHAMBRA

Built on a hill, this palace-fortress is a city in itself. Massive walls and towers served to protect the exquisite chambers and luxurious courtyards within. The beauty of the interior almost defies description. From the marble floors, graceful columns draw the eye upward to the ceilings. Through the artistry of the builders, such commonplace materials as stucco, plaster, and wood are converted into lacy patterns of great delicacy. It was within the walls of this luxurious palace that the fate of the Jews of Spain was decreed. On March 30, 1492, the Edict of Expulsion was signed in the Hall of the Ambassadors. This harsh decree, urged upon Ferdinand and Isabella by Tomas de Torquemada, the Grand Inquisitor, required that the Jews convert to Catholicism or leave the country within four months. As many as 160,000 Jews chose to leave, uprooting themselves from their homes and livelihoods, and leaving behind all they had built up over the centuries, rather than renounce their faith. It was also in this Hall of the Ambassadors in 1492 that Ferdinand and Isabella put their names to the agreement that sponsored the voyage of Christopher Columbus across the Atlantic to the New World. It is believed that there were several Marranos (secret Jews) aboard Columbus' vessels.

MADRID

SYNAGOGUE 3 Calle Balmes

After 1868, Jews were able to settle freely in Madrid, but it was not until the 1920s that the Jewish community was in any way organized. Madrid was the asylum for some Jewish refugees during the first World War, and again in the 1930s. On December 17, 1968, 476 years after the Jews were expelled, the first Jewish house of worship was built in Spain's capital. The synagogue, located near the Plaza de Sorolla, houses a school, community center, meeting hall, mikveh, and a kosher restaurant.

JUDERIA

The old Jewish quarters of Madrid were located along Calle de la Fe, Calle de Bailen, Plaza de Oriente, and Plaza de Lavapies.

MALAGA

The Costa del Sol, Spain's famous "sun coast," extends from Algeciras in the west, to Almeria, seventy-two miles of picturesque shoreline hugging the Mediterranean. In a park in the center of the city of Malaga (near the harbor) stands the statue of Solomon ibn Gabirol (1021-1069), the foremost Hebrew poet of Spain. The statue was erected by the municipality in 1969, to mark the 900th anniversary of the great poet's death, and was designed by the American sculptor, Reed Armstrong. By the age of sixteen, ibn Gabirol already showed signs of genius in his secular poetry about the joys of love and wine. However, he is best remembered for his relgious poems, many of which have been incorporated into the liturgy of the prayerbook. Although his reputation rested solely on his poetry, Solomon ibn Gabirol was also a great philosopher. His major philosophical work was the *Fountain of Life*.

There are approximately 1,000 Jews in Malaga today. The synagogue is located in an office building at 4 Duquesa de Parcent. There are regular religious services conducted at this location. There is also a Hebrew school in the building.

MALLORCA (MAJORCA)

MONTESION CHURCH

This church was built on the foundations of the Great Synagogue of Palma and has been used for centuries almost exclusively by the Chuetas. The Chuetas are descendants of Jews who were forcibly converted in 1435. Although they have been practicing Catholics for more than 500 years, they have remained, for the most part, a separate sect. They live in Palma and many own jewelry shops on the Calle de las Platerias (Street of the silver shops). The word 'Chueta' is derived from *Chuya* "pork eater" since the Chuetas ate pork publicly to demonstrate their adherence to Christianity. The local merchants call the Chuetas *Judios* or *Hebreos*.

PALMA CATHEDRAL

Among the treasures of this cathedral, which was built in 1239, are a handsome pair of 14th century *rimonim*, silver Torah ornaments. For many years these were carried aloft on poles in church processions. Even more impressive is the giant candelabrum suspended from the vaulted ceiling of the cathedral. This elegant candelabrum came from the Great Synagogue of Palma. It contains 350 lights and is a poignant reminder of the grandeur of the ancient Jewish house of worship.

MARBELLA

Many Jews are involved in the tourist industry along the Costa del Sol. There is a modest facility for worship in Torremolinos and a beautiful new synagogue building in the tract of villas called Urbanizacion El Real on the outskirts of Marbella. This small synagogue has an interesting history.The large Ohayon family built the synagogue to serve their own religious needs and those of other Jews in the area. The *Congregation Beth El*, as it is called, is the first synagogue in Spain with a Hebrew (and Spanish) inscription on its facade. Its universal message, taken from the Psalms, reads, "My house shall be called a house of prayer for all people."

SEGOVIA

CHURCH OF CORPUS CHRISTI

Originally the main synagogue of Segovia, it was converted into a church in 1420 because, as the plaque explains, the Jews allegedly desecrated the Host. The structure was built in the 13th century, designed in the Mudejar style, and resembles the Santa Maria La Blanca, in Toledo. In 1572, the building became the property of Franciscan nuns, and was very seriously damaged by fire in 1899. It has since been restored.

CALLE DE LA JUDERIA, CALLE DE LA JUDERIA NUEVA (BARRIO NUEVO)

Sites of the old and new Jewish quarters. The old quarter is located between the cathedral and the city's walls.

CHURCH DE LA MERCED

This was originally a synagogue.

EL FONSARIO

An ancient Jewish cemetery is said to have been in the Valley of the Clamores, below the city walls, once buttressing the Juderia.

SEVILLE

EL BARRIO DE SANTA CRUZ

Not far from the cathedral is the *Arco de Juderia* which was the gateway to the Jewish quarter of Seville. During the 14th century, there were 23 synagogues in the city serving over 7,000 Jewish families. However, in 1391, a series of violent anti-Jewish attacks took place, fomented by Ferrant Marinez, a high church official. The massacres and mass conversions obliterated Jewish life in the city. Some streets still recall the names of this once-vibrant Jewish community: *Calle de Cal,* Street of the Kahal or Congregation; *Calle de Cal Major*, Street of the Large Congregation; *Juderia Vieja*, the old Jewish quarter; *Calle de los Tintes*, Street of the dyers. The trade of tinting and dyeing was almost exclusively carried on by Jews. Several other churches in Seville were probably synagogues as well. These include: Church of Santa Maria Blanca, Convent of Madre de Dios, and the Church of Santa Cruz.

JEWISH CEMETERY

Located in the Macerena district. There are several 13th and 14th century Jewish tombstones within these Christian burial grounds.

COLUMBUS ARCHIVES—ARCHIVES OF INDIES 3 Avenida Queipo de Llano

Many of Columbus' backers were Marranos. Several of his crewmen on his voyage to the New World were reported to also have been Marranos (secret Jews). Columbus sailed his ships up the Guadalquivir River and docked at the inland port of Seville upon his triumphant return from the New World. Columbus is buried in the cathedral across the street from the Archives of Indies.

TOLEDO

Toledo has been compared to Jerusalem. The walled city is perched on a rocky cliff and its buildings are designed with golden-hued limestone. At its height, the Jewish community of Toledo was one of the largest and most influential in Spain. In the 12th century there were more than 12,000 Jews, 5 midrashim (small chapels), and 9 synagogues. Toledo was an important center of Jewish learning and literature. It was the home of the famous "school of translators" which included Jewish, Christian, and Moslem scholars. Among the many outstanding Jewish scholars and writers in Toledo were:

- Abraham ibn Ezra (1092-1167), an important grammarian and interpreter of the Bible. To this day, his commentaries accompany the text in most of the scholarly editions of the Hebrew Bible.

- Judah Halevi (ca.1086-1145), physician, philosopher, and poet. Many of his religious poems have become part of the prayerbook used in the synagogue on the High Holy Days. In his stirring poem, *Ode to Zion*, Judah Halevi voices his yearning for the Jews to return to the land of their fathers, Israel. He is also known for his philosophical treatise, the *Kusari*.

Interior view of the Santa Maria la Blanca in Toledo, Spain.

- Rabbi Asher bar Rav Yechiel (Rosh). Born in Germany in 1250, he offered to be jailed instead of his rabbi and teacher, Rabbi Meir of Rothenburg. The Rosh moved to Toledo in 1305 where he served as rabbi until his death in 1328.
- Rabbi Jacob bar Rav Asher (Tur). He came to Spain from Germany in 1305 with his father, the Rosh. His scholarly work was concerned with combining all laws discussed in the Babylonian and Jerusalem Talmuds.

SANTA MARIA LA BLANCA
Calle de los Reyes Catolicos

The oldest Jewish monument in Toledo, stands in a quiet garden in what was once the heart of the Juderia. It was built in the 13th century and was originally the Great Synagogue of Toledo. The exterior is unimpressive, however, the interior is very somber and awe-inspiring. The space measures 92 feet by 75 feet and is 41 feet in height. There are four aisles with 32 graceful octagonal pillars supporting a long vista of horseshoe-shaped arches. The elaborate capitals are molded in plaster and ornamented with pine-cone motifs. During the 13th century, Spain was covered with extensive pine forests. On the bases of some of the columns and on the pavements are ancient tiles. The door and ceiling are of larchwood. There is no women's section or gallery. The synagogue went through many re-uses. It was used as a refuge for reformed prostitutes, as a barracks and storeroom in the 1790s, as a dance hall, as a carpenter's workshop, and as a church—Santa Maria La Blanca. Even after so many centuries and desecrations, there is still an awesome and serene feeling as one enters the space. There is still one Star of David which has somehow survived to this day on the plaster frieze above the horseshoe arch, in the northwest quadrant of the building. The Santa Maria La Blanca is now a national museum.

The remains of an ancient ritual bath (mikveh) is located about 30 meters east of the Santa Maria La Blanca.

EL TRANSITO SYNAGOGUE Calle Samuel Levi

Samuel Levi Abulafia, for whom the street was named, was treasurer and close advisor to King Pedro I. In 1357, Don Pedro granted Abulafia permission to build this private chapel for his family. The El Transito Synagogue is a single-nave hall measuring 76 feet by 31 feet and is 39 feet in height. Adjoining the synagogue on the eastern side was Abulafia's private residence, which is no longer standing. Another building close by, at one time the residence of El Greco and now the El Greco Museum, was also part of Abulafia's property. An underground passage is said to exist along the outer edge of the Juderia, which was supposed to be used by both Jews and Marranos to escape persecution. Samuel Levi Abulafia's palace (site of today's El Greco Museum) had a tunnel leading to the banks of the Tagus River. Unfortunately, he did not have a chance to use it as an escape route. In 1361, King Pedro turned against Abulafia and accused him of cheating the royal exchequer. Abulafia was imprisoned in Seville and was tortured to death.

The El Transito Synagogue is considered to be the best preserved monument to the Jews of the pre-Inquisition period. The ceiling, made of cedar of Lebanon, is ornamented with Hebrew calligraphy. The filigreed plaster decorations on the walls and cornices contain Hebrew inscriptions and quotations from the Bible and from Psalms.

The eastern wall, encrusted with arabesque panels, is dominated by a rectangular, windowed niche, in front of which stand three foliated arches on slim colonettes. On the southern wall are galleries which was the women's section. The gallery along the western wall is said to have been the choir loft. Above the galleries runs the broad ornamental frieze. Above the frieze, a windowed arcade runs along the four walls of the hall. The side wall arcades contain alternating windows and blind arches. The arrangement along the eastern wall, however, is completely different; here two windows are set side by side in the center, which in both shape and position suggest the twin tablets of the law.

The panels on either side of the ark niche display elaborate inscriptions in Hebrew containing praise of King Pedro and Abulafia.

In 1492, the building was given to a military order, the Knights of Calatrava. There are Christian tombs of members of this order within the El Transito Synagogue. The Inquisition transformed the synagogue into the Church of Notre Dame, hence the name "Transito", transition. In 1550, the building became an asylum. In 1798, it was converted into barracks. In 1877, the synagogue building was declared a national monument. Adjoining the synagogue is a Museum of Sephardic Culture which was established by the Spanish government in 1971.

NOTE: Photography on the interior of the El Transito Synagogue is strictly forbidden.

Exterior view of the El Transito Synagogue in Toledo, Spain.

EL GRECO MUSEUM—CASA DE EL GRECO

A short distance from the El Transito Synagogue stands the so-called Casa de El Greco. This was the site of Samuel Halevi Abulafia's palace. The palace was replaced by several other buildings on the same site. The Casa de El Greco was built at the turn of the 20th century by Marques de Vega-Inclan and resembles a 16th century Manchego mansion.

JEWISH CEMETERY

Located on the road to the present-day Christian cemetery, behind the Instituto de Ensenanza Media, at the Cerro de la Horca.

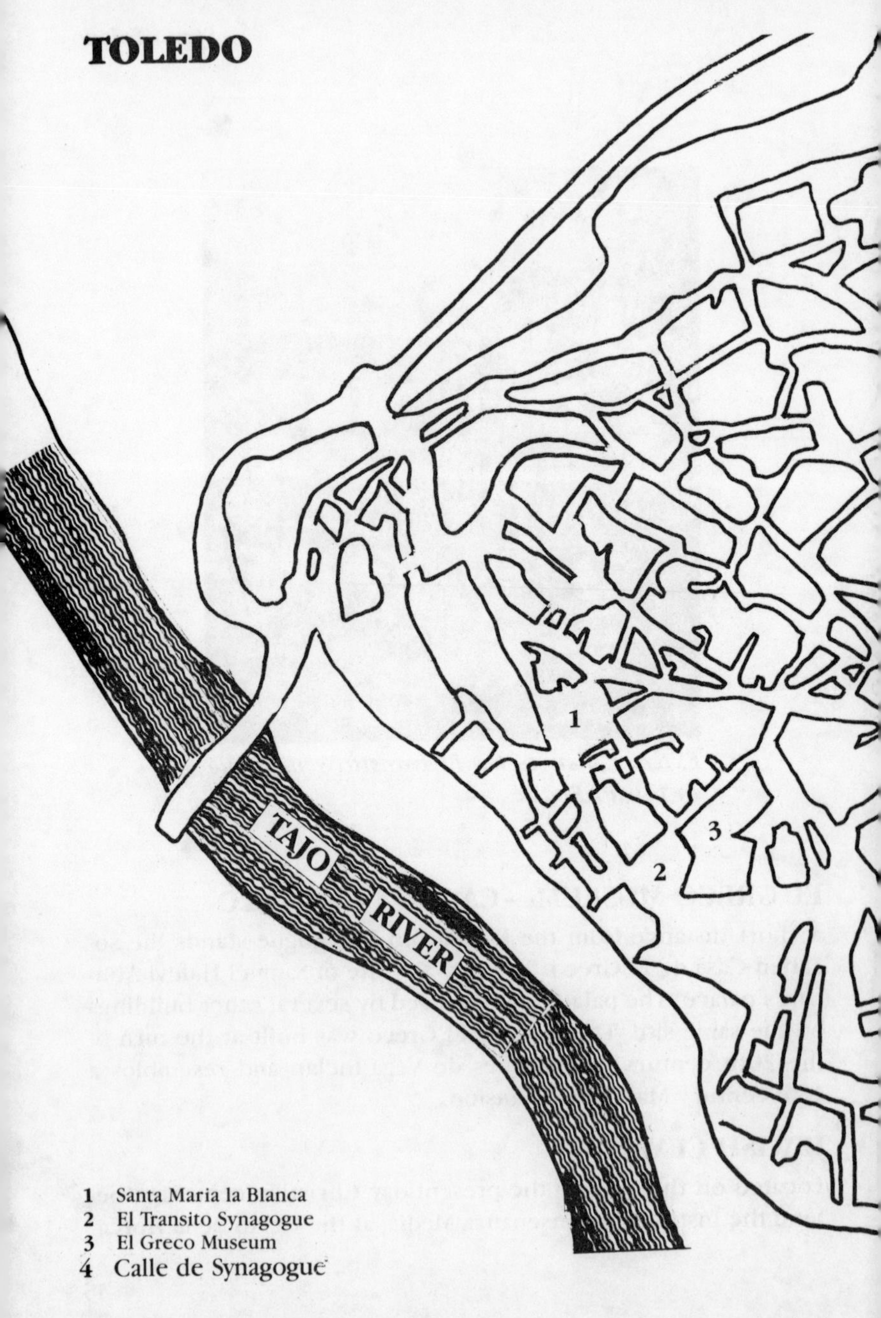
TOLEDO
TAJO
RIVER
1
2
3
1 Santa Maria la Blanca
2 El Transito Synagogue
3 El Greco Museum
4 Calle de Synagogue

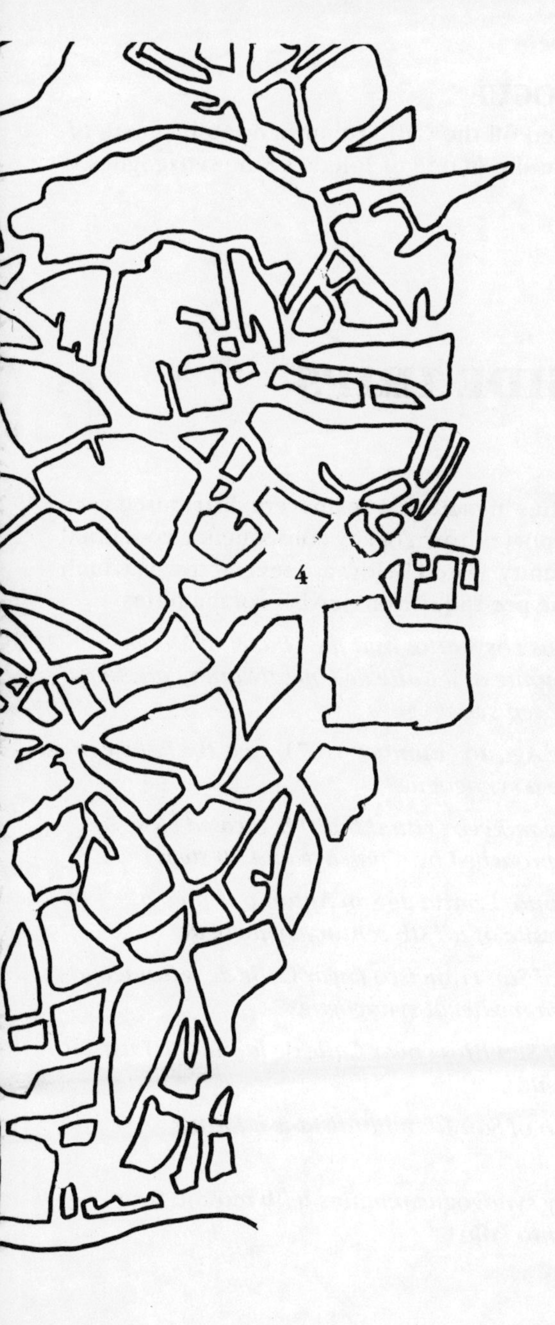
4

CALLE DE SYNAGOGUE

The small street located off the Calle Hombre de Palo (north of the cathedral), was the site of one of Toledo's nine synagogues.

SIDE TRIPS

The Jewish communities in medieval Spain were distributed very widely. Almost every port or town of any consequence contained a small Jewish community. Listed below are several towns which contain artifacts of the pre-Inquisition Jewish communities.

Avila *Church of Todos Los Santos and the Chapel of Mosen Rubi (Calle Bracamonte and Calle de Lopez Numez) are said to have originally been synagogues.*

Bejar *Calle de 29 de Agosto (number 3,5,7), near the Palace of the Dukes was once a synagogue.*

Besalu *14th century mikveh (ritual bath) is located close to the bridgehead (approached by a passage and 36 steps).*

Cacerer *Espiritu Santo, Ermita de San Antonio is now a church built on the site of a 13th century synagogue.*

Calahorra *Church of San Francisco (near Calle de le Sinagoga) built on the site of a medieval synagogue.*

Carmona *Church of San Blas (near Calle de la Juderia) was at one time a synagogue.*

Ciudad Real *Church of San Juan Bautista is a former synagogue.*

Elche *A 6th century synagogue remains with mosaic floor (near Puerta de Santo Polo)*

Estella *Church of Santa Maria Jus del Castillo was built in 1262 as a synagogue.*

Gerona *The Jewish area was located near Calle San Lorenzo. This town was the center of Kabbalism in Spain. Nachmanides (Ramban) lived in Gerona during the 13th century. The Jewish cemetery was on the hillside known as Montjuich.*

Guadalajara *Birthplace of Moses de Leon (1240-1305), author of the* Sefer Ha-Zohar. *The synagogue was located adjacent to the Church of San Pedro Y San Pablo. The cemetery was located in the vicinity of the Calle de Madrid and the Hospital Provincial. There is still a Calle de la Sinagogue.*

Hervas *Calle del Rabilero (rabbi's Street) On Calle de la Sinagogue, number 1 housed the synagogue. Casa de los Diezmos (house of the tithes) is where the Jews paid their taxes.*

Lucena *Church of Santiago is said to have been a synagogue.*

Miranda de Ebro *A medieval synagogue was preserved at 18 Calle de la Puenta. The Juderia was near the Calle de la Independencia.*

Monzon *Church of El Salvador was originally a synagogue.*

Medicaneli *Church of San Roman was originally a synagogue.*

Ona *The Juderia was on Calle Barriso (to the left of the Arch de la Estrella, towards Plaza Mayor. The second house on the right-hand side with an overhanging story was a synagogue.*

Paredes de Nava *Iglesia Cristo de la Bella Cruz was originally a synagogue.*

Siguenza *6 Calle de la Sinagoga and 12 Calle de San Vicente were original locations of medieval synagogues.*

Valencia *Church of San Cristobal on Calle del Mar was originally a synagogue.*

Vic *The Juderia and the synagogue were located between the cathedral and the Castillo de Moncada (Plaza d'en Guiu).*

Zamora *There was a medieval synagogue at number 15 Calle Ignacio Gazapo, east of the Church of Santa Lucia.*

Zaragoza *Church of San Carlos at Calle de Don Jaime I and Calle de Coso was originally a synagogue.*

SYNAGOGUES

Alicante *Calle Ramon y Cajal 9/7 (Mr. Cohen)*

Barcelona *Calle Porvenir 24 #200-61-48, #200-85-13*

Ceuta (North Africa) *Calle Sargento Coriat 8 #51-32-76*

Madrid *Calle Balmes 3 #445-95-35, #445-98-43*

Malaga *Calle Duquesa de Parcent 4 #21-40-41*

Marbella *Calle Palmera 20 #77-15-86, #77-07-57*

Melilla (North Africa) *Calle General Mola 19 #68-16-00*

Palma de Mallorca *Apartado de Correos 39 #23-86-86*

Santa Cruz de Tenerife *Calle Villalba Hervás 3 #24-77-81, #24-72-46*

Seville *Calle Peral 10 #25-81-00 ext.324*

Torremolinos (Malaga) *Calle Skal (La Roca) #38-39-52*

Valencia *Calle Ausias March 42, Puerta 35 #334-34-16*

MIKVEHS

Barcelona *Calle Porvenir 24 #200-61-48, #200-85-13*

Madrid *Calle Balmes 3 #445-95-35, #445-98-43*

Marbella *Calle Palmera 20 #77-15-86, #77-07-57*

KOSHER PROVISIONS

Madrid *(Lubavitch)* 22 Abascal *#441-5430*
Calle Balmes 3 #445-95-35, #445-98-43

Malaga *(butcher) Armengual de la Motta 20 #27-10-82*
Kosher Costa *Arango 5 #27-62-49*

Torremolinos *(butcher) Loma de Los Riscos 11 #38-79-51*

AMERICAN EXPRESS OFFICES

Alicante Viajes Melia *Esplanada Espana 5 #20-84-33*

Barcelona Passeo de Gracia (mezz.) *Chaflan Roselon #218-67-12*

Benidorm Viajes Melia *Martinez Alejos 3 #85-56-41*

Castellon Viajes Melia *#21-59-88*

Gerona Viajes Melia *San Fransisco 15 #21-94-00*

Granada Viajes Bonal *Avenida Calvo Sotelo 19 #27-63-12*

Ibiza Viajes Iberia *Avenida de Espana #30-20-14*

La Coruna Viajes Amado *Compostela 1 #22-99-72*

Lanzarote Viajes CYRASA *Carretera de las Playas (Playa, Canary Islands) #81-03-13*

Las Palmas de Gran Canaria CYRASA *Triana 114 #36-41-00*

Madrid *Plaza de las Cortes No.2 #222-11-80*

Mahon Viajes Iberia *General Goded 35 #36-29-08*

Malaga Viajes Alhambra *Plaza de las Flores S/N #21-90-90*

Palma de Mallorca Viajes Iberia *Passeig des Born 14 #22-67-43*

Puerto de la Cruz Viajes Iberia *Avenido Generalisimo Franco S/N #38-13-50*

Puerto Pollensa, Mallorca Viajes Iberia *Juan XXIII 3 #53-02-62*

Santiago de Compostella Viajes Amado *Avenido Figueroa 6 #59-36-41*

Seville Viajes Alhambra *Teniente Coronel 3 #21-29-23*

Tarragona Viajes Melia *Rambla Nova 3 #23-74-05*

Valencia Viajes Melia *Calle Paz 41 #352-26-42*

Vigo Viajes Amado *Carral 17 #21-60-21*

YOUTH HOSTELS

Barcelona *Paseig Pujades 29*
Paseo Ntra. Sra. del Coll 42 #213-86-33
Numancia 149 #230-16-06

Ceuto (North Africa) *Plaza Vieja 171 #51-51-49*

Granada *Camino de Ronda 171 #27-26-38*

Madrid *Calle Sta.Cruz de Marcenado 28 #247-45-32*
Casa de Campo #463-56-99

Malaga *Pza. Pio XII S/N Mediterraneo #30-85-00*

Mallorca *Calle Costa Brava 13 #26-08-92*

Marbella *Calle Trapiche #77-14-91*

San Sebastion *Ciudad Deportina Anoeta #45-29-70*

Segovia *Conde Sepulveda 2 #42-02-26*

Toledo *Castillo de San Servando #22-45-54*

Torremolinos *Avda Carloth Alexandre 127 #38-08-82*

Valencia *Avda. del Puerto 69 #369-01-52*

Zaragoza *Francoy Lopez 4*

RAILROAD TIMETABLES

Madrid to:

Algeciras (with connecting ferry service to Tangiers, Morocco and Gibraltar) .... 19.56—9.30

Madrid to:

Barcelona .... 11.10—20.00
Geneva .... 8.00—8.53 (next day)
Lisbon .... 10.15—19.05
Marseille .... 22.40—16.39
Nice .... 22.40—20.09
Paris .... 8.00—23.21
Rome .... 8.00—20.05 (next day)

Gibraltar

This fortified limestone promontory, known as the "Rock of Gibraltar," is situated off the southern tip of Spain. It is now a British crown colony. Jews lived in Gibraltar in the 14th century when it was a Moorish city and became a temporary haven during their flight from the Inquisition of Spain. They later continued across the Mediterranean to the North African, Moslem countries, when Spain captured the Rock in 1462. The present-day Jewish community dates from 1704, when England captured the Rock. During the Napoleonic wars, Aaron Nunez Cardozo was one of the foremost citizens of Gibraltar. His house on the Almeida subsequently became the City Hall. In the middle of the 19th century, when the Rock was at the height of its importance as a British naval and military base, the Jewish community numbered about 2,000. Most of the retail trade was in their hands. During World War II, almost all of the civilian population, including the Jews, were evacuated to British territories, and not all returned. Today there are about 600 Jews, mostly of North African origin. Some are of English ancestry, some from Eastern Europe, and a few from Israel. There are four (Sephardic) synagogues which are all functioning. Many of the stores along Main Street are Jewish owned. All of the Jewish shops are closed on the Sabbath. There is a Hebrew school, mikveh, and a kosher restaurant. In short, Gibraltar has an active Jewish community. Sir Joshua A. Hassan became the first Jewish mayor and Chief Minister of Gibraltar in 1964.

There is an *eruv* in the center if Gibraltar.

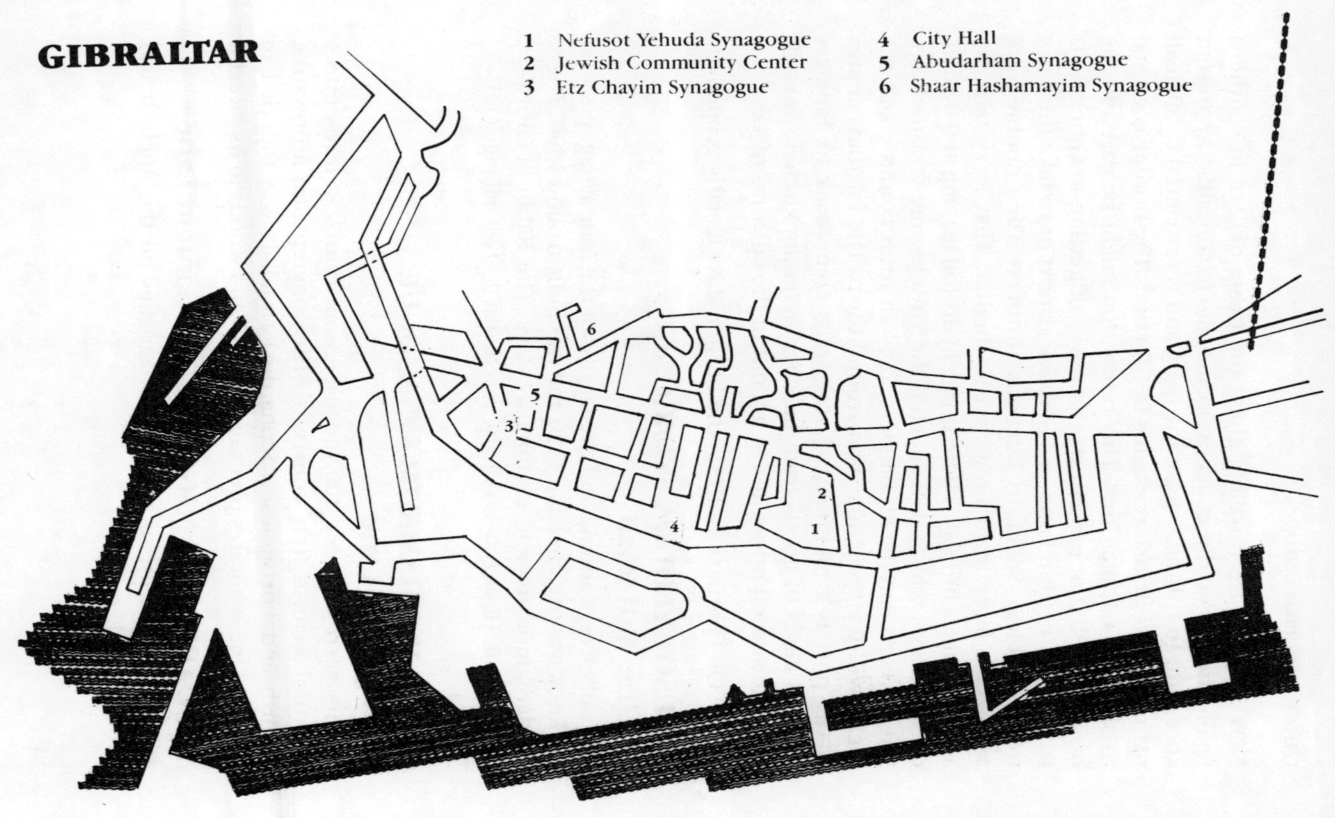
GIBRALTAR
1 Nefusot Yehuda Synagogue
2 Jewish Community Center
3 Etz Chayim Synagogue
4 City Hall
5 Abudarham Synagogue
6 Shaar Hashamayim Synagogue
6
5
3
4
2
1

NOTE: If you are traveling along the Costa del Sol in southern Spain, there is no direct access from Spain to Gibraltar. At present accession to Gibraltar from the mainland is restricted to Spanish nationals and British residents in Gibraltar. The border is closed to all other nationalities. This restriction might be eased in the near future but at present the only way of getting to Gibraltar is to fly directly from London's Gatwick airport or to take the ferry from Algeciras, Spain, to Tangiers, Morocco. Then double back and take a ferry from Tangiers to Gibraltar. That ferry trip can actually take a full day. There is one hydrofoil leaving at 9.00 a.m. on weekdays, which will shorten the voyage-time considerably. But be very careful in Tangiers. It is an Arab country and the locals will try to "guide" you around town. The customs center at the port is a nightmare. Local Arabs come back to Tangiers with all kinds of goods from Europe, including kitchen sinks! It can take several hours just to get out of the customs office.

NOTE: On February 5, 1985, the border was officially reopened.

NEFUSOT YEHUDA SYNAGOGUE
66 Line Wall Road

The only free-standing and the largest of the four synagogues on the Rock was organized in 1799 and was built around 1890. There are daily morning and evening services. The Rabbi of Gibraltar is Rabbi R. Hassett, who can be reached at 27 Town Range (tel. 77102).

SHAAR HASHAMAYIM SYNAGOGUE
47 Engineer Lane

In this narrow street, the inconspicuous doorway leads into a beautiful Spanish-style courtyard. The congregation follows the Spanish and Portuguese (Sephardic) ritual. It was founded in 1748 and incorporates precious marbles and woods in its interior.

ABUDARHAM SYNAGOGUE Parliament Lane

This is the newest of the four synagogues on the Rock. It was built in 1820.

ETZ CHAYIM SYNAGOGUE 91 Irishtown Lane

This is the oldest synagogue in Gibraltar, built in 1759. It is located upstairs, off a side-street entrance and has a seating capacity of about 75. It is almost like a *beit hamedrash* (small chapel), compared to the three other congregations in Gibraltar.

JEWISH COMMUNITY CENTER
7 Bomb House Lane

Located around the corner from the Nefusot Yehuda Synagogue, the community center houses the Hebrew school, a mikveh, communal offices, and a kosher restaurant. For information about the Jewish community of Gibraltar call 743-12

Interior view of the Spanish and Portuguese synagogue in Gibraltar.

OLD JEWISH CEMETERY

Take the cable car up the Rock. Halfway up, stop and see the famous Gibraltar apes, which were brought by the Moors from North Africa. Continue on the cable car up to the top of the Rock. Walk to the right, towards St. Michael's Caves. St. Michael's Caves is a series of cavernous tunnels with spectacular stalagtite and stalagmite formations as well as an underground lake. It is said that the tunnels under the Rock of Gibraltar continue below the Mediterranean Sea, all the way to North Africa, about twenty miles away. St. Michael's Caves were used by the Allies during World War II as a bomb-proof hospital and air-raid shelter.

As you continue southward past St. Michael's Caves, you pass the highest point on the Rock (1398m). Nearby, is the Jew's Gate which is the entrance to the old Jewish cemetery. It contains the graves of many saintly men, including that of the revered Rabbi H.M.Benaim.

CITY HALL McIntosh Square

Originally the home of Aaron Nunez Cardozo, a Jewish envoy and a friend of Lord Nelson. It is located at Linewall Road and McIntosh Square.

KOSHER PROVISIONS

Gibraltar Amar Bakery *Linewall Road (one block from the Nefusot Yehuda Synagogue)*
(butcher) McIntosh Square 26

AMERICAN EXPRESS OFFICE

Gibraltar Sterling Travel Ltd. *18 McIntosh Square* *#71787*

Portugal

Portugal's rulers between the 13th and 15th centuries were tolerant of the Jews. They opened their borders to the Jewish refugees from the massacres in Spain in 1391 and its Inquisition of 1492. In 1531, however, Portugal issued its own Inquisition. The Jews were given eight months to leave Portugal. Many headed for nearby North Africa while others moved to Holland and its colonies in the New World. Many Marranos stayed in Portugal. Their descendents are today concentrated in the northern provinces of Tras-os-Montes, Beira Alta, and Entre-Douro-e-Minho. It is common to find Marrano families lighting Friday evening candles, although they have no idea that these were originally meant to be Sabbath candles. They claim that it has been a family tradition to light candles every Friday evening. There are about 300 Jews, not including Marranos, in Portugal today.

LISBON

RUA DA JUDIARIA

This was part of the 15th century Jewish quarter.

SYNAGOGA SHAARE TIKVA
59 Rua Alexandre Herculano

The Sephardic synagogue of Lisbon was built in 1902 and was designed in Moorish-Revival style.

PORTO

KADOORIE SYNAGOGUE
340 Rua Guerra Junqueiro

Kahal Kodesh Mekor Haim Synagogue was built by the Kadoorie family (of Bagdad) in the 1920s.

TOMAR

MEDIEVAL SYNAGOGUE Rua Nova

Located in the old Jewish quarter, this former synagogue was used as a wine cellar for centuries and is now a national landmark.

FARO

JEWISH CEMETERY

A 14th century Jewish cemetery is located in this southern Portuguese port city.

SYNAGOGUES

Lisbon *(Sephardic) 59 Rua Alexandre Herculano #6815-92 (Ashkenazic) 110 Rua Elia Garcia #7752-83*

Porto *340 Rua Guerra Junqueiro*

KOSHER PROVISIONS

Lisbon Rabbi Abraham Assor *Rua Rodrigo da Fonseca 38-1 DTO #53-03-96*

Porto Rua Rodrigues *Lobo 98 #65535*

(butcher) Rua da Escola Politechnica 279 #652450

AMERICAN EXPRESS OFFICES

Estoril Star Travel Service *Avenida de Nice 4 #268-08-39*

Faro Star Travel Service *Rua Conselheiro Bivar 36 #25-125*

Funchal (Madeira) Star Travel Service *Avenida Arraiga 23 #32001*

Lisbon Star Travel Service *Avenida Sidinio Pais 4-a #53-98-41*

Star Travel Service *Praca dos Restoradores 14 #362-501*

Porto Star Travel Service *Avenida dos Aliados 202 #23-637*

Portimao Star Travel Service *Rua Judice Biker 26A #25-031*

YOUTH HOSTELS

Lisbon *Rua Andrade Corvo 46 #53-26-96*
Estrada Marginal #243-06-38

RAILROAD TIMETABLES

Lisbon to:

Bordeaux	15.10–14.10
Faro	8.10–12.55
Madrid	7.30–18.40
Paris	15.10–19.15 (next day)

France

There is evidence of Jewish settlement in ancient Gaul (today's France) dating back to the 4th century. The period between the 9th and 12th century marked a Golden Age for French Jewry. It was the era of the great rabbis and their world-renowned rabbinical academies. It was a period of cultural awakening, producing great scholars and poets. The first known scholar was Rabenu Gershom ben Judah (ca.960-1030), who later was known as the *Meor ha-Golah*, the light of the Diaspora. He was responsible for issuing special ordinances (*takkanot*) which were designed to raise the level of morality. The most widely known of these *takkanot*, forbids polygamy. The achievements of Rabenu Gershom were continued by his disciple, Rabbi Shlomo Yitzchaki, generally known by his Hebrew acronym "Rashi." Though he studied in Worms, Germany, he was born, worked, and died in Troyes, France (1040-1105).

From the 11th century through the 18th century, there were very explosive periods for the Jews. The first major upheaval occurred in 1096, with the First Crusade. The Christians aimed their attacks against the Jews living in the provinces which bordered the Rhine River. There were persecutions based on the accusation of "ritual murders." In 1240, the church condemned the writings of the Jews and publicly burnt editions of the Talmud. There were retaliatory expeditions organized by religious fanatics who accused the Jews of being the cause of the general poverty. In 1348, during the epidemic of the Black Plague, which

FRANCE

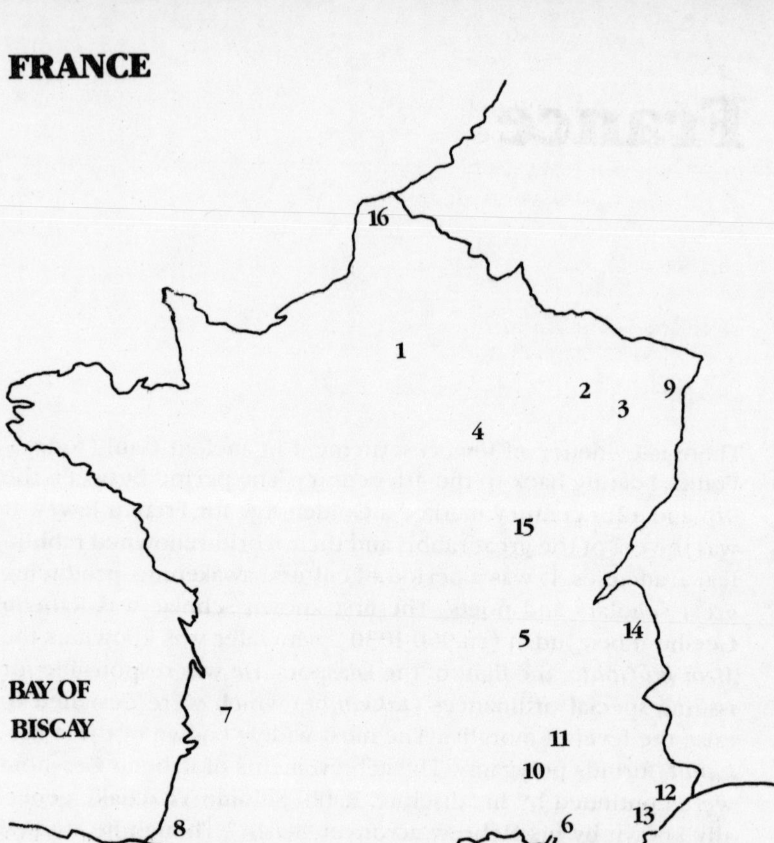

1	Paris	9	Strasbourg
2	Luneville	10	Avignon
3	Saarebourg	11	Carpentras
4	Troyes	12	Nice
5	Lyon	13	Cannes
6	Marseille	14	Chamonix
7	Bordeaux	15	Dijon
8	Biarritz	16	Dunkerque

took the lives of over one third of the population of Europe, some twenty-four million people, Jews were burned at the stake in many Alsatian towns, a persecution which is still commemorated in the name of several streets, especially in Strasbourg. During these massacres, the most heroic among the Jews committed collective suicide while others converted to Christianity.

In 1394, Charles VI expelled all Jews from France. This decree did not include Alsace, Comtat Venaissin (Provence), and the County of Nice. It was not until 1784 that Jews were to return and settle in all parts of France. In 1791, the Jews were proclaimed full citizens of France. Napoleon assembled 71 Jewish leaders as a *Sanhedrin* in 1806, which was to clarify the Jewish attitude on the subject of the relations between church and state. This body was the forerunner of today's Consistorial system.

Many Jews achieved fame in France after the French Revolution. In art, great names include Pissaro, Soutine, Bonheur, Pascin, Chagall, and Modigliani. Musical enrichment came from Jacques Offenbach, Claude Kahan, and Darius Milhaud. In literature and the humanities, Nobel Prize winners were Henri Bergson and Rene Cassin; notables in finance were the Rothschilds; in government, three French prime ministers, Leon Blum, Rene Meyer, and Pierre Mendes-France.

During World War II, the world witnessed the deportation of 100,000 French Jews. In the 1960s there was a major influx of Jews from the North African countries of Algeria, Morocco, and Tunisia. These Sephardic Jews would move into the old and dying Jewish communities throughout France and virtually bring them back to life. Today, there are about 750,000 Jews in France, with 385,000 residing in Paris. There are more than 200 synagogues and about 50 kosher restaurants. There are also 25 Jewish day schools, several Jewish magazines and newspapers, and even a half-dozen free radio networks.

PARIS

(Paris Metro stations in brackets)

THE PLETZEL

Metro #1 (Saint Paul)

Located on the site of the 13th century ghetto of Paris, known as the *juiverie*, the Pletzel (Yiddish term for "little place") is still an active Jewish section. Jews have lived and worked for many centuries in these narrow streets. At one time, place Saint Paul was known as "Jews' Place." At the turn of this century, the area was populated mostly by Eastern European Jews and had a similar atmosphere as New York City's Lower East Side at the turn of the century. Yiddish was heard on the streets of the quarter and most of the signs on the stores were printed in Yiddish as well. Since the second World War most of the old Ashkenazic shops have been replaced with Sephardic and Oriental ones. This was due to the mass influx of North African Jews in the mid-1960s. The language and signs are now in Hebrew and French.

The Pletzel's most famous street is rue des Rosiers. Other streets in the area include: rue Pavee, rue des Hospitalieres—Saint Gervais, rue des Ecouffes, rue Ferdinand—Duval, and rue Geoffroy—l'Asmer. The famous Jo Goldenberg restaurant is located on rue des Rosiers. It is not a kosher restaurant. It is kosher style. There is memorial plaque honoring the victims of a terrorist attack in this restaurant which occurred in July, 1982.

MEMORIAL OF THE UNKNOWN JEWISH MARTYR 17 rue Geoffroy-l'Asnier

Metro #7(Pont-Marie)

One of the most moving Jewish memorials in Paris is a tribute to the six million Jews who perished in the Holocaust. It was dedicated in October, 1956. A huge bronze cylinder in the center of the courtyard is designed in a shape symbolizing a crematorium urn. The museum contains documents and photographs of World War II. It is open daily, except Saturday, from 10.00 a.m. to 12 noon and from 2.00 p.m. to 5.30 p.m. For further information call 227-44-71

MEMORIAL TO THE DEPORTED

Metro #4 (Cité)

Located in a garden behind Notre Dame Cathedral on the tip of the Ile de la Cité, not far from the Pletzel. This memorial is dedicated to the 200,000 French men and women of all races and religions who died in the German death camps during World War II. It was designed by architect Georges-Henri Pingusson in 1962.

CONSISTOIRE OF PARIS 17 rue Saint-Georges

Metro #7 (le Peletier)

This is the headquarters of the Jewish community of Paris, officially known as the Association Consistoriale Israelite de Paris. It was created by an ordinance of May 25, 1844, which fixed the compositions of the consistories. For information about the Jewish community of Paris call 526-02-56

TEMPLE VICTOIRE 44 rue de la Victoire

Metro #7 (le Peletier)

This austere and magnificent building is often called the "cathedral" and "Rothschild" synagogue. It was built in 1874, in the days of Napolean III, in the Romanesque Revival style. It was designed by Alfred Philibert Aldrophe, one of the foremost architects of France, and who was at that time the chief architect of the city of Paris. The synagogue is lavishly decorated with marble and stained- glass and is dominated by glorious candelabras. The two chairs on either side of the ark are reserved for the chief rabbi of France and the chief rabbi of Paris. For further information about services call 285-71-09.

PARIS

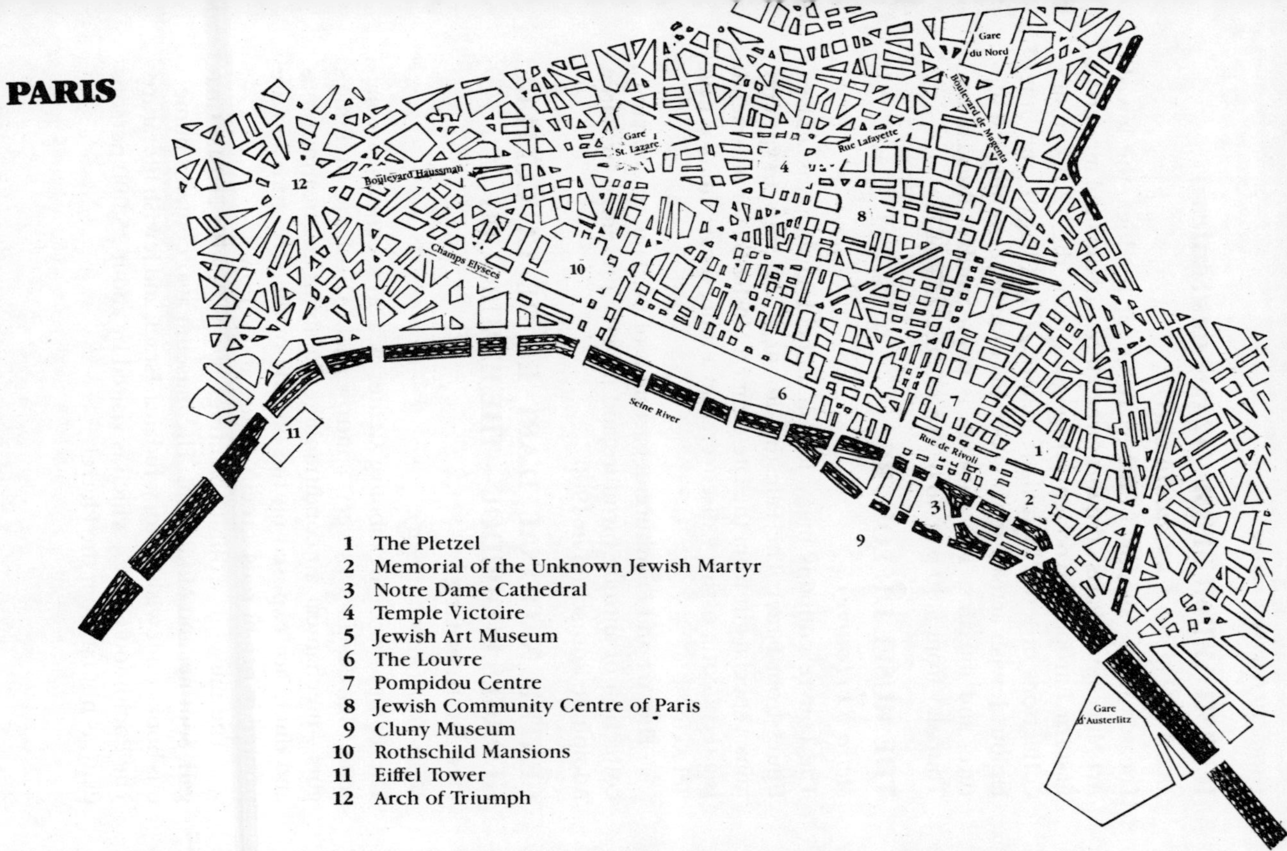
Gare du Nord
Boulevard de Magenta
Rue Lafayette
Gare St. Lazare
Boulevard Haussman
Champs Elysees
Seine River
Rue de Rivoli
Gare d'Austerlitz
1 The Pletzel
2 Memorial of the Unknown Jewish Martyr
3 Notre Dame Cathedral
4 Temple Victoire
5 Jewish Art Museum
6 The Louvre
7 Pompidou Centre
8 Jewish Community Centre of Paris
9 Cluny Museum
10 Rothschild Mansions
11 Eiffel Tower
12 Arch of Triumph

JEWISH ART MUSEUM 42 rue des Saules

Metro #12 (Lamarck-Caulaincourt)

Located in the shadow of the Sacre Coeur Basillica, the Jewish Art Museum of Paris contains rare exhibits of detailed models of Eastern European wooden synagogues from the 12th century, collections of Jewish ritual art, paintings by Chagall, and other famous Jewish artists. It also contains drawings, etchings, sculpture, and mosaics. The museum is open Sunday, Tuesday, and Thursday from 3.00 p.m. to 6.00 p.m. (tel. 257-84-15)

THE MUSEE DU LOUVRE

Metro #1 (Louvre)

The Louvre contains many Jewish archeological items and antiques from Israel. The Palestine Room of the Sully Crypt contains a special gift from the late General Moshe Dayan of Israel. It is a terra cotta ossuary discovered in a funeral cave in Azor near Tel Aviv.

The Art and Furniture department of the Louvre contains a collection of antique furniture and jewelry presented by Baron Adolph de Rothschild in 1900.

CENTRE NATIONAL D'ART ET DE LA CULTURE GEORGES POMPIDOU—THE BEAUBOURG rue Beaubourg

Metro #11 (Rambutteau)

The Pompidou or Beaubourg Center is a 21st century art museum. Its design was very controversial. All of the building's guts—mechanical, air conditioning , plumbing, and heating pipes and ducts are exposed on the outside of the structure and are painted in bright reds, greens, blues, and yellows!

The museum exhibits paintings by the Jewish artists: Chagall, Soutine, and Modigliani. The museum also contains numerous books on Jewish history, Judaica, Israel, and Jewish literature. The Pompidou Center, which is visited by about 25,000 persons daily, is not far from the Pletzel.

JEWISH COMMUNITY CENTER
19 boulevard Poissonniere

Metro #8 or #9 (rue Montmartre)

There are dances, movies, classes, some sports, Saturday evening socials for singles, and Wednesday evening Israeli folk dancing. The center also houses a kosher cafeteria and serves lunches from 12 noon to 2.00 p.m. There is a synagogue on the premises. For further information call 233-64-96.

As you walk along the rue Montmartre, you will notice many kosher restaurants and snack bars, which are mostly owned by Sephardic Jews from North Africa. Continue to rue Richer, which is world renowned for its Follies Bergeres (no.32), but also notice the kosher restaurant right next door to the Follies!

MUSEE DE CLUNY 6 place Paul Painleve

Metro #10 (Saint Michel)

The Cluny Museum contains the Strauss–Rothschild collection of Jewish ritual objects. There are Jewish engagement rings, sculptures, and attached to the wall, are a series of stone slabs which were originally 13th century Jewish tombstones. There is also an inscribed cupboard ark and a reading desk, which have come from a 15th century synagogue in Modena, Italy.

ROTHSCHILD MANSIONS

Metro #9 (St. Phillipe du Roule)

There are several exquisite mansions which, at one time, belonged to several members of the Rothschild family. They are located along rue du Faubourg-St.-Honore, at numbers: 33, 35, 41, 45, and 49.

LUNÉVILLE

The synagogue built between 1785 and 1789 at Lunéville reflects the elegance of 18th century France. Its facade, like that of a small but very superior urban residence, is ornamented with a discreetly Judaic symbol entirely in keeping with Neo-Classical taste—festoons of vine leaves and grapes.

Exterior view of the elegant synagogue at Luneville, France.

SAAREBOURG

There were periods in French Jewish history when the Jews were restricted in their design of the synagogue. It was not to be a tall structure (taller than the cathedral). The Jews wanted to subdue their synagogue design by having the building "blend-in" with the neighboring structures. At times these synagogues resembled barns and were actually known as *stahl* or barn synagogues. This camouflaged appearance might one day actually save the synagogue from angry mobs during pogroms. The Saarebourg synagogue was built in 1858 on the site of an earlier and smaller building. The exterior looks similar to the adjoining barn. During World War II, the Nazis used the synagogue as a warehouse. The interior, having been restored after the war, is a gem, complete with its marble ark, exquisite stained-glass windows, and brass candelabras.

STRASBOURG

Jewish history in Strasbourg goes back to the 12th century. There were savage persecutions during the Crusades and many massacres over the centuries. From the 14th century to the French Revolution, Jews were not permitted to live in Strasbourg. Rue Brulee memorializes the massacre of February 13, 1349, when 2,000 Jews were burnt in a huge bonfire for refusing to accept baptism. The city of Strasbourg today is known as the "Jerusalem of France." It is an active and highly organized intellectual Jewish community which has supplied many of the chief rabbis of France. Today, there are about 12,000 Jews living in Strasbourg.

ALSATIAN MUSEUM 23 quai St. Nicolas

This museum has a rich collection of Jewish ritual objects displayed in three rooms on the main floor. This collection belongs to the Jewish museum.

SYNAGOGUE DE LA PAIX (SYNAGOGUE OF PEACE) 1A rue du Grand Rabbin Rene Hirschler

The main synagogue, replacing the one destroyed by the Nazis during World War II, was built in 1958. It was designed by architect Meyer Levy. Twelve sixty-foot high columns support the segment-arched copper barrel roof. Seating capacity is seventeen hundred. The ark, a cylindrical structure with a conical roof, is derived from the shape of the rolled-up scroll of the Law. The various types of wood from former French Africa are used in the doors and fittings. The southern aisle of the hall of worship leads out into an open pillared portico, which overlooks a beautiful public park. A bronze menorah and a bronze grating shaped in the pattern of a Magen David grace the front of the structure. There are two additional chapels in the adjoining community center; one is used by a Sephardic congregation. There is a kosher restaurant on the first floor of the building which is open from 8.00 a.m. to 3.00 p.m. (tel. 36-56-30)

SIDE TRIPS

- There are beautiful historic synagogues in Dijon, Bordeaux, Biarritz, Haguenau, and Colmar.
- For a truly breathtaking and unforgetable journey, take the cable car over Mont Blanc, Europe's tallest mountain

(15,772ft.), from Chamonix, France, to Courmayeur, Italy (only during the summer months). You must have your passport since you will be crossing the French-Italian border. You can continue to Turin by train or bus which is about one and one half hours away.

- If you are going from Paris to Marseille, you should take the T.G.V., Europe's fastest train. It is not as fast as Japan's "Bullet Train" but it does go up to a speed of 165mph and will get you there in about five hours, instead of the usual seven hours. On the way down to Marseille, be sure to stop-off in the beautiful city of Lyon. There is a Jewish community numbering about 20,000. There are 20 synagogues, several kosher restaurants, 16 kosher butcher shops, a day school and 13 talmud torahs.

PROVENCE

In the southern part of France in the medieval period, groups of Jews lived in the "four holy communities": Avignon, Carpentras, Cavaillon, and l'Isle-sur-Sorgue, in what was then papal territory. It was to this region where the Pope had been exiled in the 14th century. Jews in this region spoke the Provençal dialect and adhered to the Sephardic ritual, adding a special liturgy of their own, called *comtadin*, which greatly resembled Portuguese. Living under the direct jurisdiction of the Popes, they fared better than the Jews in the rest of France. This does not mean, however, that they escaped arbitrary restrictions and expulsions directed at other Jews in France. The Jews served as financiers and merchants. No medieval synagogues have survived in France, but two 18th century synagogue buildings at Carpentras and Cavaillon were restored following World War II and declared national monuments. Today, they are maintained as museums as well as functioning synagogues.

CARPENTRAS

SYNAGOGUE place de la Synagogue

Originally built in 1367, but was remodelled in 1741 by architect Antoine d'Alemand. He originally had planned to construct the remodelled building 72 feet high. The church authorities were opposed to this height since it would be taller than both the Church of the White Penitents and the Cathedral of St. Suffrein. The walls of the synagogue were not to exceed 42 feet in height and the eastern windows which faced the church were walled up.

The synagogue is decorated in the delicate style of salons in the reign of Louis XV. The layout of the synagogue is quite unique. The ark is on the main level along the eastern wall. On the right side of the ark, standing in a niche six feet above the floor, is a miniature Chair of Elijah. Decorated with appropriate inscriptions, the chair is symbolic of the Prophet Elijah protecting the new-born male child on the day of his circumcision. There was no *bimah* or reading platform on the main level but rather, it was placed on the upper gallery, on the western wall, and was reached by two sets of winding stairs on each side of the supporting Tuscan columns. In the original 1367 synagogue building, the women were placed in the cellar. There was a special rabbi or cantor who conducted the service for the women. The basement also housed a matzoh bakery, complete with oven, grindstone, and a marble kneading table dated 1652. On an even lower level was a mikveh, the *cabussadou* as is it called in the Provençal dialect. HOW TO GET THERE: From Avignon, take the bus which stops directly in front of the railroad station (on the main street). Ride to the last stop, about a 40-minute ride, and ask for the synagogue. It is opposite the town hall.

The Carpentras Synagogue is open every day from 10.00 a.m. to 12 noon and from 3.00 p.m. to 5.00 p.m. There are daily and

Chair of Elijah in the ancient synagogue at Carpentras, France.

Sabbath services. There are about 100 families, the majority coming from North African Jewish communities in the 1960s.

There is another ancient synagogue and museum in the nearby village of Cavaillon. It is very similar in design to the synagogue of Carpentras but contains much greater art works, especially its delicate wrought-iron grilles and sculpted medallions. The synagogue is located at rue Hebraique, between rue Chabran and rue de la Republique. The museum is open from 10.00 a.m. to 12 noon and from 2.00 p.m. to 5.00 p.m., everyday except Tuesday. If the building is closed, contact Mr. Mathon at 23 rue Chabran or Mr.Palombo at 36 rue Raspail (tel. 78-02-46).

MARSEILLE

The area stretching from Marseille to Menton is known as the French Riviera. There have been Jews in Marseille since Roman times. This port city was the center for Jewish merchants and traders shipping their goods to the Near and Far East lands. There are today about 70,000 Jews living in Marseille. There are about 25 synagogues, several day schools, and kosher restaurants.

NICE

There were Jews living in Nice as early as the 4th century. In 1723, there was a ghetto in the heart of the old city. It is said that the house at 18 rue Benoit Bunico was originally an ancient synagogue. There are today eight synagogues in Nice, which has a Jewish population of about 25,000. The largest of the synagogues is located at 7 rue Gustave Deloye. It was built ca. 1890 and follows the Sephardic ritual. The exquisite ark is designed as a walk-in area and contains twelve Torahs. During the summer season the synagogue is packed—standing room only!

You will notice French policemen standing near all synagogues throughout France during Friday evening and Sabbath services. This has been the official policy since the terrorist attacks against synagogues several years ago. On some streets there are police barricades as well. These are designed to block all vehicular traffic through that street during the services. It has been noted by the rabbis of many synagogues throughout Europe that it is highly advisable to leave the synagogue area or courtyards as soon as the services finish and not 'hang-around' to wait for or meet with people. This is a very simple security measure which should be adhered to.

There is a small Ashkenazic synagogue just around the corner at 1 rue Blacas.

NATIONAL MUSEUM BIBLICAL MESSAGE OF MARC CHAGALL
Docteur Menard avenue & Cimiez boulevard

The most important permanent collection ever assembled and devoted to Marc Chagall. The museum includes large paintings, preparatory sketches, gouaches, and engravings. There are also lithographs, sculptures, stained-glass, and tapestries. For further information call tel. 81-75-75.

CANNES

The city known for its film festival and fireworks displays (nightly, in mid-August) has a Jewish population of about 10,000. There is a synagogue at 19 boulevard d'Alsace and a kosher butcher. There is a kosher cafeteria in the Jewish Community Center at 3 rue de Bone (tel. 99-24-95).

MONACO—MONTE CARLO

There is a synagogue at 15 avenue de la Costa and a kosher butcher at 70 avenue Saint Laurent (tel. 30-11-73).

NOTE: If you are planning to be in the French Riviera during the month of August, it will be extremely crowded. August is the month in which all of Europe goes on vacation.

SYNAGOGUES

Agen *52 rue Montesquieu #96-17-79*

Aix-en-Provence *3 rue de Jerusalem #26-69-39*

Amiens *38 rue du Port d'Amont #89-66-30*

Annency *18 rue de Narvick #67-69-37*

Antibes Villa la Monada *Chemin des Sables #61-59-34*

Arcachon Cours Desbey *(summers only)*

Avignon *2 place de Jerusalem #25-12-92*

Bayonne *35 rue Maubec #55-85-59*

Belfort *6 rue de l'As de Carreau #28-55-41*

Besançon *2 rue Mayence #80-82-82*

Beziers *19 place Pierre Semard #28-75-98*

Biarritz *rue de Russie #55-85-59 (High Holy Days only)*

Bischeim *place de la Synagogue #33-02-87*

Bitche *28 rue de Sarreguemines*

Bordeaux *8 rue du Grand Rabbin Joseph Cohen #91-70-39*

Boulay *rue du Pressoir #779-20-34*

Brest *8 quai de la Douane #45-98-42*

Caen *46 avenue de la Liberation #93-46-32*

Cannes *19 boulevard d'Alsace #38-16-54*

Carpentras *place de la Synagogue*

Cavaillon *rue Hebraique #78-02-46*

Chalon-sur-Marne *21 rue Lochet #68-09-92*

Chalon-sur-Saone *10 rue Germigny #48-05-41*

Clermont-Ferrand *6 rue Blatin #93-36-59*

Colmar *1 rue de la Cigogne #41-38-29*

Creil *1 place de la Synagogue #425-16-37*

Dijon *5 rue de la Synagogue #66-46-47*

Dunkerque *19 rue Jean Bart #66-92-66*

Elbeuf *rue Gremont #81-19-61*

Epernay *2 rue Placet #51-26-83*

Epinal *9 rue Charlet #82-25-23*

Frejus Saint-Raphael *rue du Progres #40-20-30*

Grenoble *11 rue Andre Maginot #87-02-80*

Haguenau *rue du Grand Rabbin Joseph Bloch #93-87-24*

le Havre *38 rue Victor Hugo #21-14-59*

le Mans *4 boulevard Paixhans #31-99-55*

Lens *87 rue Casimir Beugnet #28-22-14*

Libourne *33 rue Lamothe #51-45-99*

Lille *5 rue August Angelliers #52-41-59*

Limoges *25 rue Pierre Leroux #77-47-26*

Lunéville *5 rue Castara #373-08-07*

Lyon *16 rue Saint Mathieu #800-72-50*
la Sauvegarde + la Duchere #835-14-44
317 rue Duguesclin #858-18-74
13 quai Tilsitt #837-13-43
47 rue Montesquieu
60 rue Crillon
11 rue Saint Catherine

Marseille *119 rue Breteuil (6e) #37-49-64*
8 impasse Dragon (6e) #53-33-73
24 rue Montgrand #33-61-79
14 rue Saint Dominique (1e) #39-64-30
31 avenue des Olives (13e) #70-05-45
57 boulevard Barry (13e) #66-13-15
134 boulevard Michelet (9e)

27 boulevard Bonifay (10e) #89-40-62
18 rue Beaumont (1e) #50-30-57
205 boulevard Saint Marguerite (9e) #75-63-50
15 avenue des 3 Freres Carasso (4e) #66-40-89
20 chemin Saint Marthe (14e) #62-70-42
60 chemin Vallon de Toulouse (10e) #75-14-97

Menton *1 bis avenue Thiers #57-79-52*

Metz *39 rue du Rabbin Elie Bloch #775-04-44*

Monaco *15 avenue de la Costa #30-16-46*

Montpelier *5 rue des Augustins #60-49-93*

Mulhouse *19 rue de la Synagogue #45-85-41*

Nancy *17 boulevard Joffre #332-10-67*

Nantes *5 impasse Copernic #73-48-92*

Nice *7 rue Gustave Deloye #85-44-35*
1 rue Blacas

Paris (Metro station in brackets followed by Paris districts.)
44 rue de la Victoire (le Peletier) 9e
21 bis rue des Tournelles (Bastille) 4e
12 rue des Saules (Lamarck-Caulaincourt) 18e
120 boulevard de Belleville (Belleville) 20e
14 rue Chasseloup Laubat (Cambronne) 15e
13 rue Saint Isaure (Jules-Joffrin) 18e
19 boulevard Poisonnieres 2e
13 rue Fondary 15e
14 place des Vosges 4e
75 rue Julien Lacroix (Menilmontant) 20e
9 rue Vanquelin (Censier Daubenton) 5e
70 avenue Secretan (Bolivar) 19e
15 rue Notre Dame de Nazereth (Temple) 3e
28 rue Buffault (Cadet) 9e

ORTHODOX
10 rue Cadet (Cadet) 9e

31 rue de Montevideo (Pompe) 16e
10 rue Pavee (Saint Paul) 4e
6 rue Ambroise Thomas 9e
4 rue Saulinier (Montmartre) 9e
32 rue Basfroi (Voltaire) 11e
25 rue des Rosiers (Saint Paul) 4e
24 rue du Bourg Tibourg (Hotel de Ville) 4e
80 rue Doudeauville (Chateau Rouge) 18e
5 rue Duc (Jules-Joffrin) 18e
9 passage Kuszner (Bellville) 19e
18 rue des Ecouffes (Saint Paul) 4e
21 rue de Turenne (Chemin Vert) 4e
18 rue Saint Lazare 9e
84 rue de la Roquette (Voltaire) 11e

LIBERAL

24 rue Copernic (Victor Hugo) 16e

NOTE: There are an additional 75 synagogues in the suburbs surrounding Paris.

Pau *8 rue des Trois Freres Bernadac #62-37-85*

Perigueux *13 rue Paul Louis Courrier #09-57-50*

Perpignan *54 rue Arago #34-75-81*

Reims *49 rue Clovis #47-68-47*

Roanne *9 rue Beaulien #71-51-56*

Rouen *55 rue des Bons Enfants #71-01-44*

Saarebourg *12 rue du Sauvage #703-12-67*

Sarreguemines *rue Georges V #798-20-48*

St. Etienne *34 rue d'Arcole #33-09-18*

St. Fons *17 avenue Albert Thomas #867-39-78*

St. Quentin *11 ter boulevard Henri Martin #62-17-36*

Selestat *4 rue Saint Barbe #92-04-35*

Sete *quai d'Orient #53-24-13*

Strasbourg *1a rue Rene Hirschler #35-61-35*
2 rue St. Pierre le Jeune
rue d'Istanbul
6 rue de Champagne
rue Rieth
28 rue Kageneck
1 rue Silbermann

Tarbes Cite Rothschild *6 rue du Pradeau #93-04-74*

Thionville *31 avenue Clemenceau #253-23-23*

Toulon *6 rue de la Visitation #91-61-05*

Toulouse *14 rue du Rempart, St. Etienne #21-69-56*
2 rue Palaprat #62-90-41
17 rue Alsace Lorraine #21-51-14
35 rue Rembrandt
3 rue Jules Chaland
8 rue Etienne Colongues Colomiers

Tours *37 rue Parmentier #05-56-95*

Troyes *5 rue Brunneval #43-11-02*

Valence *1 place du Colombier #43-34-43*

Valenciennes *36 rue de l'Intendence #33-49-13*

Verdun *impasse des Jacobins #84-30-51*

Versailles *10 rue Albert Joly #951-05-35*

Vichy *2 bis rue du Marechal Foch #98-44-02*

Villeurbanne *4 rue Malherbe #884-04-32*

MIKVEHS

Aix-en-Provence *3 rue de Jerusalem #26-69-39*

Aix-les-Bains *rue Roosevelt (Pavilion Salvador) #35-38-08*

Avignon *rue Guillaume #85-21-24, 25-12-92*

Bordeaux *213 rue St.Catherine #91-79-39*

Colmar *3 rue de la Cigogne #41-38-29*

Dijon *5 rue de la Synagogue #65-35-78*

Grenoble *11 rue Andre Maginot #87-02-80*

Haguenau *7 rue Neuve*

Lens *58 rue du Wets #28-16-16*

Lyon *18 rue Saint Mathieu #800-72-50*
317 rue Duguesclin #858-18-74
40 rue Alexandre Boutin #824-38-91

Marseille Colel 43a Ch. Vallon de Toulouse (10e) #75-28-64
Longchamp *45a rue Consolat (1e) #62-42-61*
Redon *13 boulevard du Redon (9e) #75-58-49*
Beth Myriam *60 Chemin Vallon de Toulouse #75-20-98*

Metz *rue Kellerman #775-04-44, 775-14-93*

Mulhouse *19 rue de la Synagogue #45-85-41*

Nantes *5 Impasse Copernic #73-48-92*

Nice *22 rue Michelet #85-34-84, 80-58-96*

Nimes *40 rue Roussy #23-11-72*

Paris *9 rue Villehardouin (3e) #887-59-69*
50 Faubourg St.Martin (10e) #206-43-95
7 rue du Bourg l'Abbe (3e) #272-33-99

Saint Louis Institut Messilath Yesharim *Vielle route de Hagenthal #68-51-77*

Sarreguemines *rue Georges V #798-20-48*

Strasbourg *1a rue Rene Hirschler #36-43-68*

Toulon *6 rue de la Visitation #91-61-05*

Toulouse *15 rue Francisque Sarcey #21-20-32*

Troyes *5 rue Brunnevalid #43-11-02*

Paris *176 rue du Temple #271-89-28*

KOSHER RESTAURANTS

Bordeaux Cafeteria Henri IV *89 rue Henri IV #92-74-90*

Grenoble Maison Communitaire *11 rue Andre Maginot #87-02-80*

Lyon Lippmann *4 rue Tony Tollet #842-49-82*

(bakery) 2 rue jubin

Marseille le Mont Carmel *5 rue de l'Arc #33-42-13*

Pitapain Tchick-Tchack *65 rue d'Augagne #54-45-33*

Metz Galil *39 avenue Elie Bloch #775-04-44*

Nice Restaurant Universitaire Kosher *31 avenue Henri Barbusse #51-43-63*

Chez David Guez *26 rue Pertinax #85-70-16 (Sabbath meals by reservation only)*

Tikva *rue du Suisse*

Nimes Centre Communitaire *5 rue d'Angouleme (only Wednesday afternoons)*

Paris Aux Surprises *40 bis Faubourg Poissoniere (10e) #770-24-19*

Azar *39 rue Richer (9e) #246-31-39*

New Boules *8 rue Geoffroy Marie (9e)* #246-39-56

Centre Communitaire *19 boulevard Poissoniere (2e) #233-80-21. (Open Monday—Friday from 12 noon to 2.00 p.m.) Sabbath meals available—by prior reservations only.*

Centre Rachi *(for students and visiting adults) 30 boulevard Port Royal (5e) #331-98-20. (Closed July 15—September 15)*

le Chandelier *4 rue Paul Valery (16e) #704-55-22. (Reservations advisable for this first-class strictly kosher restaurant which is housed in an 18th century mansion. Open 12.30 p.m. to 2.00 p.m and 7.30 p.m. to 10.00 p.m. except Friday and Saturday.)*

Chez Raphael *12 rue Geoffroy Marie (9e) #770-39-43*

Dar Djerba *110 boulevard de Belleville #797-25-32*

Faraj Freres *39 rue Richer (9e) #246-03-73*

Foyer Israelite *5 rue de Medicis (6e) #326-58-30*

Jasmin de Tunis *79 boulevard de Belleville #806-23-03*

Jo Goldenberg *7 rue des Rosiers (4e) #887-20-16. (This restaurant is not kosher but serves kosher-style meals.)*

Chez Claude *35 rue Bergere (9e) #770-77-09*

la Boule de Neige *1&3 rue de la Grange—Bateliere*

la Relais *69 boulevard de Belleville (11e) #357-83-91. (Open 12 noon to 2.30 p.m. and 6.30 p.m. to 9.00 p.m. Closed on Saturday.)*

l'Onec *2 rue Ambroise Thomas (9e) #523-48-60*

Milk Chic *56 rue Richer (9e) #770-24-19*

Rose Blanche *10 bis Rue Geoffroy Marie #523-37-70*

Restaurant Vietnamin *54 rue des Rosiers (4e)* #427-82-309

Shalom *10 rue Richer (9e) #246-77-70*

Sidi bou Said *2 rue de la Grange Bateliere #770-03-98*

Restaurant Universitaire *5 rue de Medicis (6e) #326-58-30*

Violin sur le Tiot *16 rue Thorel #236-27-26*

Yhalot *24 rue des Rosiers (4e) #272-30-43*

Zazou Freres *19 rue du Faubourg de Montmartre #770-80-63*
Tibi *128 boulevard de Clichy (18e) #522-96-99*
a la Bonne Bouchee *1 rue Hospitalieres Saint Gervais (4e) #508-86-02*
Adolphe *14 rue Richer (9e) #770-91-25*
l'Oneg *2 rue Ambroise Thomas (9e) #523-48-60*
Gagou *8 rue de la Grange Bateliere (9e) #770-05-02*
Centre Edmond Fleg *8 bis rue de l'Eperon (6e) #633-43-24. Lunch only from 12 noon to 2.00 p.m. (closed August)*
le Cesaree *20 rue de la Verrerie (4e) #272-23-81*

Strasbourg Centre Communitaire *1 rue du Grand Rabbin Rene Hirschler #36-56-30*
Le Domino 28 rue Sellenick #(88) 35-15-04
Aladin 6 rue du Faubourg de Pierre #22-38-70

Restaurant Universitaire *11 rue Sellenick #35-15-68. (Open for visitors from July to September only.)*

AMERICAN EXPRESS OFFICES

Cannes *8 rue des Belges #38-15-87*

le Havre *57 quai Georges V #42-59-11*

Lourdes Office Catholique de Voyages *14 Chausse de Bourg #94-20-84*

Lyon *9 rue Childebert #837-40-69*

Nice *11 Promenade des Anglais #87-29-82*

Paris *11 rue Scribe #266-0999*
83 bis rue de Courcelles #766-0300

11 place du Marche, le Vesinet #976-5039
38 avenue de Wagram #227-5880

Rouen *1/3 place Jacques Lelieur #98-19-80*

St. Jean de Luz Socoa Voyages *31 boulevard Thiers #26-06-27*

YOUTH HOSTELS

Biarritz *19 route des Vignes #63-86-49*

Bordeaux *22 cours Barbey #91-59-51*

Chamonix *les Pelerins #53-14-52*

Colmar *7 rue St. Niklaas #41-33-08*

Dijon *1 boulevard Champollion #71-32-12*

Grenoble *avenue du Gresivaudan #09-33-52*

Lyon *51 rue Roger Salengro #876-39-23*

Marseille *47 avenue J. Vidal #73-21-81*

Menton *plateau St. Michel #35-93-14*

Nice *route Forestiere du Mont Alban #89-23-64*

Paris *8 boulevard Jules Ferry #357-5560*
125 avenue de Villeneuve,St Georges #890-9230
4 rue des Marguerites #749-4397
33 boulevard Jourdan
444 rue de la Division Leclerc #632-17-43

Strasbourg *9 rue de l'Auberge de Jeunesse #30-26-46*

Toulouse *125 avenue Jean Rieux #80-49-93*

RAILROAD TIMETABLES

Paris to:

Destination	Times
Amsterdam	10.23—16.34
Barcelona	9.33—23.31
Berlin	7.30—20.46
Copenhagen	7.30—22.45
Frankfurt	9.00—15.13
Lisbon	9.00—9.55 (next day)
London	7.55—13.50
Madrid	20.00—8.55
Marseille	10.11—15.06
Nice	10.11—18.05
Rome	7.34—23.55
Stockholm	7.30—8.17 (next day)
Venice	7.18—19.34
Vienna	7.45—22.50
Zurich	7.00—13.57

Italy

Italian Jewry is the oldest Jewish community of the European Diaspora. Its origins go back to 139 B.C.E. to the Roman Republic. From then on, Jewish connections with Italy and especially, with Rome, have been virtually uninterrupted to the present day. Large numbers of Jewish prisoners of war were brought to Rome after the destruction of the Temple in Jerusalem in the year 70. The Arch of Titus, in the ruins of the Roman Forum, commemorates this event with a bas relief showing the Jewish slaves carrying the spoils of the Temple; the *menorah*, the *shulchan* , and the silver trumpets.

There were large Jewish centers throughout southern Italy, especially in Sicily, until 1492, at which time the Inquisition caught up with the Jews and witnessed their expulsion. The Jews then resettled to the northern provinces.

The Jews of Italy were at the mercies of the Popes. Edicts against Jews were issued periodically. Pope Innocent III, in the 13th century, ordered that all Jews must be distinguishable from Christians and decreed that men must wear a bright yellow circle on their garments and women must have two blue stripes on their shawls. The Jews of Italy were later also required to wear a bright red velvet hat. In 1516, the first ghetto in Italy was established, in Venice. The Jews were forced to live within a limited and enclosed space. They were permitted to work outside the ghetto walls during the day, but at sunset, all Jews were required to return. The last of the ghettos to be dismantled was in Rome, in 1870.

ITALY

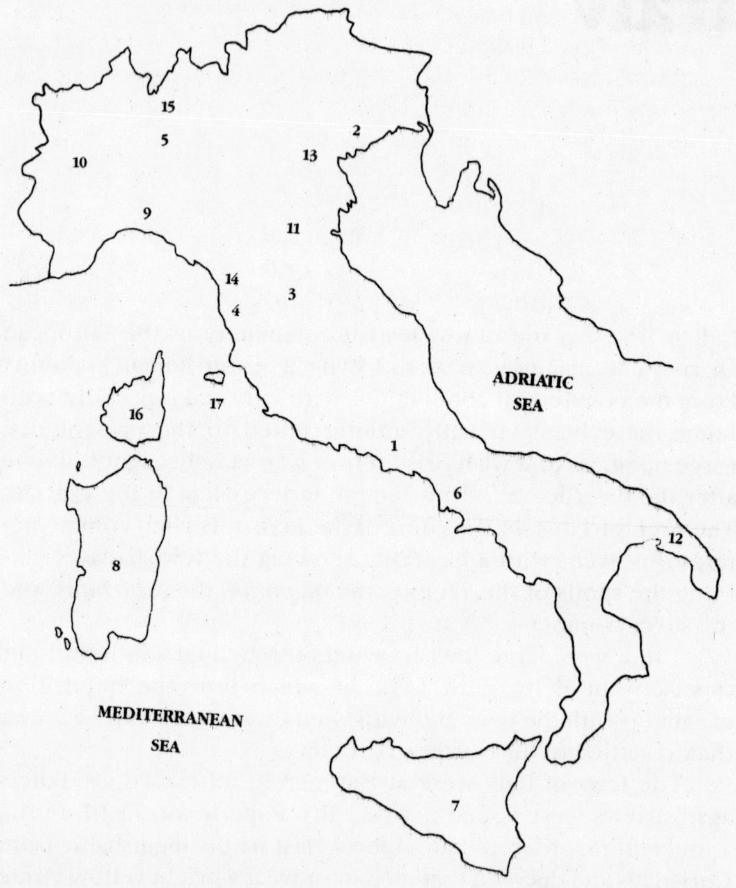

1	Rome	10	Turin
2	Venice	11	Bologna
3	Florence	12	Brindisi
4	Leghorn	13	Padua
5	Milan	14	Pisa
6	Naples	15	Como
7	Sicily	16	Corsica (French)
8	Sardinia	17	Elba
9	Genoa		

The Renaissance period of the 15th and 16th centuries was a cultural peak for Italian Jewry. Jews were physicians, scientists, and artists. They studied simultaneously rabbinical lore and the writings of classical antiquity, and taught the Bible and dancing, Hebrew grammar, and Italian poetry, all in complete harmony.

Some personalities of this period include:

- Leone de Modena (1571-1648)—rabbi, scholar, poet, and author of thirty-five books.
- Gershom Soncino—printer of Hebrew books around 1500.
- Solom ben Azariah de' Rossi (ca.1600)—known as the "father of modern Jewish music," composer of Renaissance madrigals, symphonies, and Jewish liturgical music.

On March 29, 1848, Carlo Alberto, King of Sardinia, extended civil rights to all Jews of Italy. Jews now entered every avenue of life in the new Italy. Some occupied high public office while many were distinguished writers, scholars, scientists, and jurists. During World War II, the Italians did not comply with the Nazis in "handing over" the Jews. The synagogues were not destroyed by the Nazis, however, in 1943, some 10,000 Italian Jews were deported to the Nazi death camps. Today, there are about 30,000 Jews living in Italy.

ROME

TEMPLE OF DIVO GIULIO

Erected on the spot where the body of Julius Caesar, in whom the Jews had found so much sympathy and support, had been cremated. The Roman historian Sventonius reports that, out of devotion, the Jews kept a vigil at Caesar's funeral pyre for a number of consecutive nights, and even half a century later, they still showed their mourning before the mausoleum of Augustus.

ARCH OF TITUS

Built in the year 81 by Emperor Domitian, the Arch of Titus commemorates the destruction of the Holy Temple of Jerusalem in the year 70 by Titus Vespasianus Augustus. There is a bas relief under the arch depicting Jewish slaves carrying the loot from the Temple including the *menorah, shulchan,* and the silver trumpets. The Talmud places a prohibition against Jews from walking under the Arch of Titus. The Arch of Titus is located at the beginning of Via Sacra.

THE COLOSSEUM

The amphitheatre begun by the Emperor Vespasian in the year 72 and completed by his son Titus in 80. Many Jewish slaves, brought to Rome after the destruction of the Holy Temple in Jerusalem, were used for its construction.

MAMERTINE PRISON

Built in the 2nd century, the Mamertine Prison was used as a state prison and a place used for capital executions. The prison is below street level. The prisoners were hurled into it through two holes in the ceiling. It was there that Aristobolus II, deposed king of Judea and, in the year 70, Shimon bar Giora, defender of the city of Jerusalem against the legions of Titus, were imprisoned.

THE GHETTO

The ghetto of Rome was established as an act against the Reformation by the Protestants against the Catholic church. The Popes believed that the Jews were rebelling against the church as well. On July 12,1555, Pope Paul IV established the ghetto of Rome. Located near the present-day Great Synagogue of Rome, the ghetto contained 130 tenement houses which were divided between two large and six small streets. The ghetto covered an area of one third of a square mile and housed 10,000 Jews. There

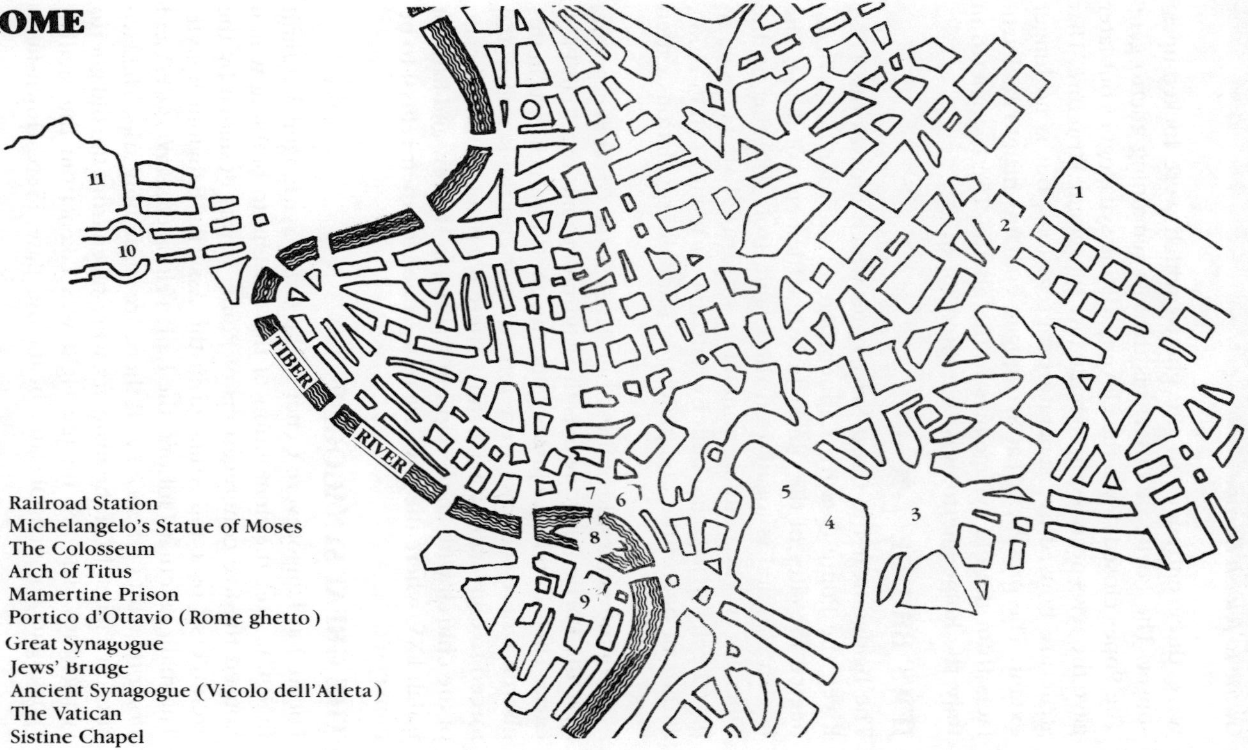

ROME

1 Railroad Station
2 Michelangelo's Statue of Moses
3 The Colosseum
4 Arch of Titus
5 Mamertine Prison
6 Portico d'Ottavio (Rome ghetto)
7 Great Synagogue
8 Jews' Bridge
9 Ancient Synagogue (Vicolo dell'Atleta)
10 The Vatican
11 Sistine Chapel

were three entrances to the ghetto which were locked-up at sunset. The Portico d'Ottavio is the last remaining ghetto gate. The Popes closed down the eleven existing synagogues but later gave the Jews permission to build one synagogue structure. That structure housed five separate congregations, but is no longer extant. The present Great Synagogue contains many ritual artifacts from the old synagogues of the ghetto. The last ghetto in Italy, the Rome ghetto, was "liberated" in 1870.

JEWS' BRIDGE

The bridge near the Great Synagogue which crosses the Tiber River, the Ponte Quattro Capi (bridge of the four heads) connected the sites of the oldest Jewish settlements of Rome. The Jewish Hospital is located on the island, Isola Tiberina, in the Tiber River. The building at number 13 Via Dell'Atleta is said to have been a synagogue built by Nathan ben Yechiel (1035-1106), author of one of the compendia of Talmudic regulations called "*sefer arukh.*"

On the same side of the Tiber River as the Great Synagogue, near the Portico d'Ottavio, is the Church of Sant'Angelo in Prescaria. This church was just outside the ghetto walls. It was in this church where the Jews were forced to attend the sermons and forced to convert to Christianity. There is a plaque on the facade of the church with an inscription written in Hebrew and Latin of Isaiah LXV, where the Jews are reproached for their refusal to be converted.

THE GREAT SYNAGOGUE

Located at Lungotevere Cenci 9, the Great Synagogue was built in 1904, after the demolition of the old ghetto building which housed the five congregations of Rome. It was designed by the architects Costa and Armanni in the Assyrian-Babylonian style. The main sanctuary follows the Italian ritual (*nusach italki*) and along the east (*mizrach*) wall there are three holy arks. The two arks on each side of the main ark were taken from the old ghetto synagogues. The ark on the right was taken from the Sicilian Synagogue (or School) and bears the date 1586. Downstairs, there is an additional synagogue with an ark removed from the Spanish School. The services conducted downstairs follow the Spanish ritual. For the past several years, there has been a major rehabilitation project in the main sanctuary. There is presently a mesh of scaffolding filling the entire room. Nevertheless, services still continue in the main sanctuary. There is a Jewish Museum adjoining the main sanctuary. Some of the magnificent items of the museum include: antique plaques from the catacombs of Via Portuense and from the ancient 3rd century synagogue at Ostia Antica, silver Torah ornaments, the actual Papal Bull issued in 1555 by Pope Paul IV "*cum nimis absurdum*," ordering the Jews to live in a ghetto, and a glorious gilded "chair of Elijah," used during circumcisions, dating from the 16th century. Museum hours are: Monday through Friday , 10.00 a.m. to 2.00 p.m. and on Sunday, 10.00 a.m. to 12 noon. The museum is closed on Saturday. For further information call 65-64-648. There are daily services in the Great Synagogue. For synagogue services information call 65-50-51.

NOTE: There is a strict security check before entering the Great Synagogue building. Several years ago there were terrorist attacks against the Jewish community. Today there are armed police and security agents standing watch at all Jewish centers. Photography inside the synagogue building is strictly forbidden.

THE VATICAN

St. Peter's contains a column which is said to have been taken from the Holy Temple in Jerusalem. The column is located on the right side of the "Pieta" Chapel of Michelangelo. It has been recorded by Benjamin of Tudela, that during his visit to Rome in the 12th century, the Jews of that city told him that on the eve of *Tish'a Ba'av*, the ninth day of the Hebrew month of Av which commemorates the destruction of both Holy Temples in Jerusalem, that sacred column in the Vatican weeps. It was that twisted column which inspired Bernini to design the Baldachino of the High Altar in St. Peter's.

The ceiling of the Sistine Chapel was created by the famous

artist, Michelangelo, in 1512. Michelangelo depicts a series of biblical scenes: the separation of light from darkness, the creation of trees and plants, the creation of man, the creation of Eve, the fall of man, the sacrifice of Noah, the flood, and the drunkenness of Noah.

MICHELANGELO'S MOSES

In the Church of St. Peter in Chains (San Pietro in Vincoli), stands the great sculpture of Moses. It was created in the 16th century and depicts Moses with horns emanating from his head. This was due to a misinterpretation of a verse in the Bible (Exodus 34:35), where the word "*keren*" is translated as "horn" instead of "ray of light." It is said that the Jews of Rome would flock out of the ghetto on Saturday afternoons and watch Michelangelo work on this sculpture.

OSTIA ANTICA

During the construction of the highway near Rome International Airport in 1961, the archeological remains of a 3rd century synagogue in the ancient seaport of Ostia were discovered. Two architraves, each with a sculptured menorah, lulav, shofar, and etrog were proof that this ancient ruin was originally a synagogue. There was an entrance with three doorways facing southeastward, toward Jerusalem. There was a mikveh, an oven used for baking unleavened bread (matzoh) for Passover, and a small yeshiva adjoining the synagogue. HOW TO GET THERE: Take the Rome subway towards Ostia and get off the train at Ostia Antica. The archeological park is open daily (except Monday) from 10.00 a.m to 5.00 p.m.

The city of Ostia is a local beach resort. There are many Russian Jews living in Ostia.

VENICE

Jewish traders and merchants from the Ashkenazic (German) lands were living in Venice as early as 1290. They lived on the island opposite San Marco, originally called Spinlunga but later known as Giudecca, "Island of the Jews." At one point, there were synagogues on Giudecca but it is said that they were demolished in the 18th century. The Jews were also involved in money-lending and created pawnbroker shops throughout the city. The Jews of Venice were not permitted to own houses or real estate and were required to wear a yellow badge or red velvet hat to be distinguished from the Christian population. In 1516, the first ghetto in the world was created. It did not expel the Jews from the city but rather, the edict gave the Jews in Venice ten days to move into the old abandoned munitions foundry. The word "foundry" in Italian is *geto*. Initially, there were seven hundred Jews living in the ghetto but, over the next hundred years, the population swelled to five thousand. They were forced to build tenements seven stories high which were known as Venetian "skyscrapers," since all the buildings in Venice were no taller than three stories.

During the day, the Jews could circulate freely in the city. At sunset, however, they all returned into the ghetto where, during the night, the guards, paid by the Jews themselves, watched over the entrances and the canals. Although the Jews were confined to their ghetto, the 16th and 17th centuries were an age of cultural and artistic development and brought to prominence many outstanding scholars. Rabbi Leon de Modena, equally versed in religious studies and ordinary writers, was the author of many works and a popularizer of culture. Many non- Jewish scholars attended his lessons and sermons. Sara Copio Sullam a gifted poetess, was admired for her beauty and culture, and known for her literary salon which was frequented by learned men and aristocrats. It was not until Napoleon invaded Venice in 1797 that the gates of the ghetto were torn down. The Jews of Venice were then made free citizens.

VENICE GHETTO

As you leave the railroad station, turn left and walk along the Lista di Spagna until you get to a canal. Cross over the bridge and immediately turn left. Walk along the canal for about three hundred feet (just past the pier on the canal) and look for a small archway with two signs above. One sign says Hospedale Pedialrico and the other sign (yellow) is in Hebrew and Italian and says "Sinagoghe." This is the entrance to the ghetto.

Entrance to the Venice Ghetto.

VENICE GHETTO

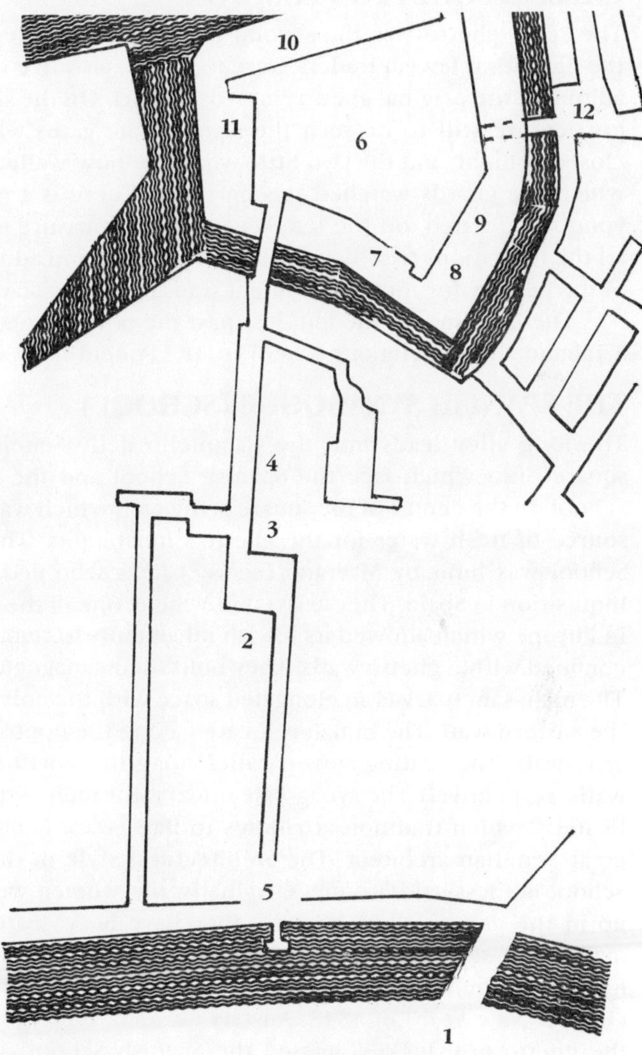

1 From Railroad Station
2 Spanish Scuola
3 Levantine Scuola
4 Midrash of Leon de Modena
5 Entrance to the Ghetto Vecchio
6 Ghetto Nuovo
7 Italian Scuola
8 Canton Scuola
9 Great German Scuola
10 Jewish Rest Home
11 Holocaust Memorial
12 Ghetto Nuovissimo

CALLE DI GHETTO VECCHIO

The "old" ghetto was the second phase of enclosure, whereby the Levantine Jewish traders were forced to also live in the area adjoining the original ghetto (nuovo) in 1541. On the sides of the portico are still to be seen the signs of the gates which were closed at night, and the two little windows, now walled up, from which the guards watched this entrance. There is a plaque beyond the portico, on the left, recalling the measure and listing all the limitations to which Jews had to submit and adding a note of the penalty for those who might transgress these laws.

The building on the left, just past the portico, once housed a Talmud Torah (religious school) of the Ponentini.

THE SPANISH SYNAGOGUE (SCHOOL)

The long alley leads into the Campiello delle Scuolo, a large square onto which face the Spanish School and the Levantine School. In the center of the square is the well which was the only source of fresh water for the ghetto's inhabitants. The Spanish School was built by Marrano (secret) Jews who fled from the Inquisition in Spain. They arrived in Venice, one of the few cities in Europe which allowed its Jewish inhabitants to remain, albeit, confined within ghetto walls. They built their synagogue in 1554. The main sanctuary is an elongated space with the holy ark along the eastern wall. The bimah is located along the opposite (western) wall. The seating runs parallel along the north and south walls, respectively.The synagogue underwent radical restoration in 1635, which tradition attributes to Baldassare Longhena, the great Venetian architect. The architectural style of the Spanish School is Classical Baroque. Originally, the women were seated up in the galleries but recently they have been seated on the main level, separated with a partition, since the upper galleries have been found to be structurally unsound. On Rosh Hashana (Jewish New Year) of 1848, Austria invaded Venice. Bombs hit the ghetto but, luckily, missed the Spanish School. There is a plaque along the bimah wall recalling this event.

The Spanish School follows the Orthodox (Sephardic) ritual.

The Ghetto of Venice.

Sabbath and Festival services are conducted in this School only during the summer months. During the remainder of the year, services are held across the square, in the Levantine School.

THE LEVANTINE SCHOOL

Across the square from the Spanish School stands the Levantine School. It was founded in 1538 by the Levantine Jews. At the entrance hall is a plaque commemorating the visit of Sir Moses Montefiore in 1875. On the right is a small study and prayer hall, the Luzzato Yeshiva. It was previously located in the Campio di Ghetto Nuovo. Going upstairs to the main synagogue, one enters into an architectural gem. Designed in the late Baroque style, the bimah is the work of Andrea Brustolon, the noted Venetian wood sculptor. There are two wide curving stairways of twelve steps, decorated by columns that outline it effectively. The pulpit appears framed by two heavily decorated twisted columns, which recall those of Solomon's Temple in Jerusalem. This synagogue is used on Sabbaths and Festivals during the winter season.

CALLE DEL FORNO

Leaving the Levantine School, one walks into a small open space, Corte Scalamata, and turns left into the Calle del Forno. This is the site of the matzoh factory—still operational today.

MIDRASH OF LEON DE MODENA

Leaving the Levantine School, turn right and walk along Ghetto Vecchio. Number 1222 was the study of the noted scholar, Leon de Modena.

On the opposite side of the street was the Midrash Vivante, which was founded in 1853.

GHETTO NUOVO

Cross over the bridge and you will arrive in the new foundry site or the Ghetto Nuovo. This was the first location in which the German and Italian Jews were confined, in 1516. The main square had three wells which served the original seven hundred ghetto inhabitants.

ITALIAN SCHOOL

This was the last synagogue built in the ghetto. It was constructed in 1575 by the Jews belonging to the Italian ritual. It was the site where the great spiritual leader, Leon de Modena, delivered his famous sermons. The building is no longer in use. You can identify the building, which seems to blend in with the adjoining structures, by looking for five large windows with a crest above the central window. There is a Baroque umbrella dome on a high polygonal drum, from which the windows illuminate the bimah beneath.

CANTON SCHOOL

This synagogue takes its name from the Canton family, the rich German bankers who built it as their private oratory of the Ashkenazic rite. It was built in 1531, but is no longer in use. It is recognized by its high wooden umbrella dome rising on an octagonal drum.

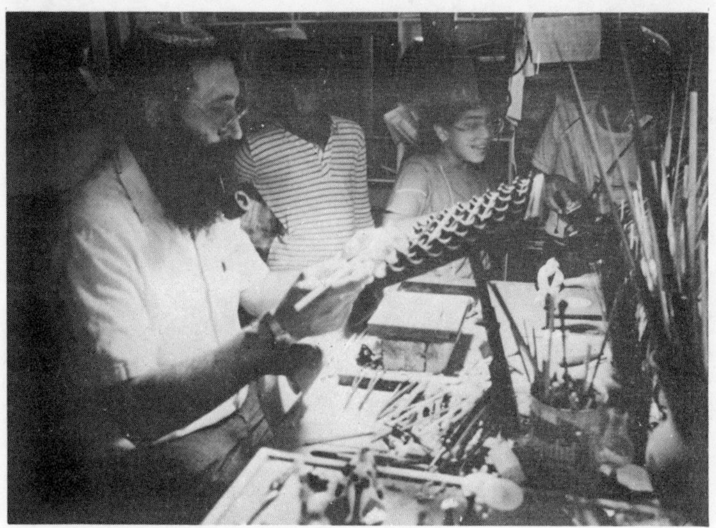

The glassblower in the Venice Ghetto.

The holy ark of the Great German School in the Venice Ghetto.

GREAT GERMAN SCHOOL

This was the first synagogue built in the ghetto. It was the German Jews who built it in 1528 for the practice of the Ashkenazic rite. The builder found it difficult to insert the plan of the synagogue in the already existing building, so its plan appears slightly asymetrical, almost trapezoidal. The exterior is recognized by its five windows, of which three are walled-up, with arches in white stone. The main features in the synagogue are the gilded ark and bimah and the elliptical women's gallery. This synagogue is no longer in use and is housed above the Museum of Jewish Art.

MUSEUM OF JEWISH ART

Housed in rooms below the Great German School, the Museum of Jewish Art was created after World War II. Some items of interest are ancient mantles for Torahs, ark covers, silver Torah crowns, a canopy (chupah) for Jewish weddings, and a chair of the prophet Elijah, used for circumcisions.

JEWISH REST HOME

There is a small chapel adjoining the Jewish Rest Home which houses a 17th century ark from the Mesullanim School, an Ashkenazic or German rite congregation which was demolished in the 19th century. This chapel is used for daily prayers. Arrangements for Sabbath afternoon meals can be made in the Jewish Rest Home on Friday. Kosher wine is also available at this location.

HOLOCAUST MEMORIAL

On the wall adjoining the Jewish Rest Home are seven sculptural memorial plaques commemorating the six million Jewish men, women, and children who perished during World War II. There were two hundred Venetian and eight thousand Italian Jews who died during the Holocaust. The memorial plaques were designed by A.Blatas. There is a similar Holocaust Memorial in New York City. It is located across the street from the United Nations, at Dag Hammarskjold Park, which was also designed by A.Blatas. The door to the right of the Holocaust Memorial is the ghetto mortuary.

GHETTO NUOVISSIMO

Leaving the museum, turn right and go through a portal. Cross a wooden bridge and turn left. This was the "newest" ghetto, which was added to the Ghetto Nuovo and Ghetto Vecchio in 1633.

JEWISH CEMETERY

There is no cemetery within the ghetto walls. Land was acquired in 1386 on the island called "Lido." At the Riviera San Nicolo 2, at the corner of Via Cipro, is the ancient Jewish cemetery. Some personalities buried in the "Cimitero Ebraico" are: Leon de Modena, Sara Copio Sullam, Simone Luzzatto, and Daniel Rodriguez.

FLORENCE

GREAT SYNAGOGUE Via L.C.Farini 4

Started in 1874, its construction took eight years and it was inaugurated on October 10,1882, after the official visit of the king of Italy. The synagogue was designed by the architectural firm of Treves, Falcini, and Mičheli in the Moorish Revival style. The building underwent two major restorations. The first, following the Nazi retreat from the city. They placed mines beneath the pillars of the synagogue. An ax-mark still appears on the door of the ark, left by the Nazi stormtroopers. The second major restoration occurred after the terrible flood of 1966. The congregation follows the Italian ritual. The interior walls and domed ceiling are finished in stenciled polychrome decorative patterns, typical of Moorish design. On the synagogue grounds are communal buildings which house the Hebrew school and mikveh. There is a kosher restaurant outside the synagogue gates at Via Farini 2a (one flight up).

STATUE OF DAVID

Created by Michelangelo in 1504, the Statue of David is housed in the Academia delle Belle Arti. A copy of the statue stands in the Piazza della Signoria, near the site of the old ghetto of Flor-

FLORENCE

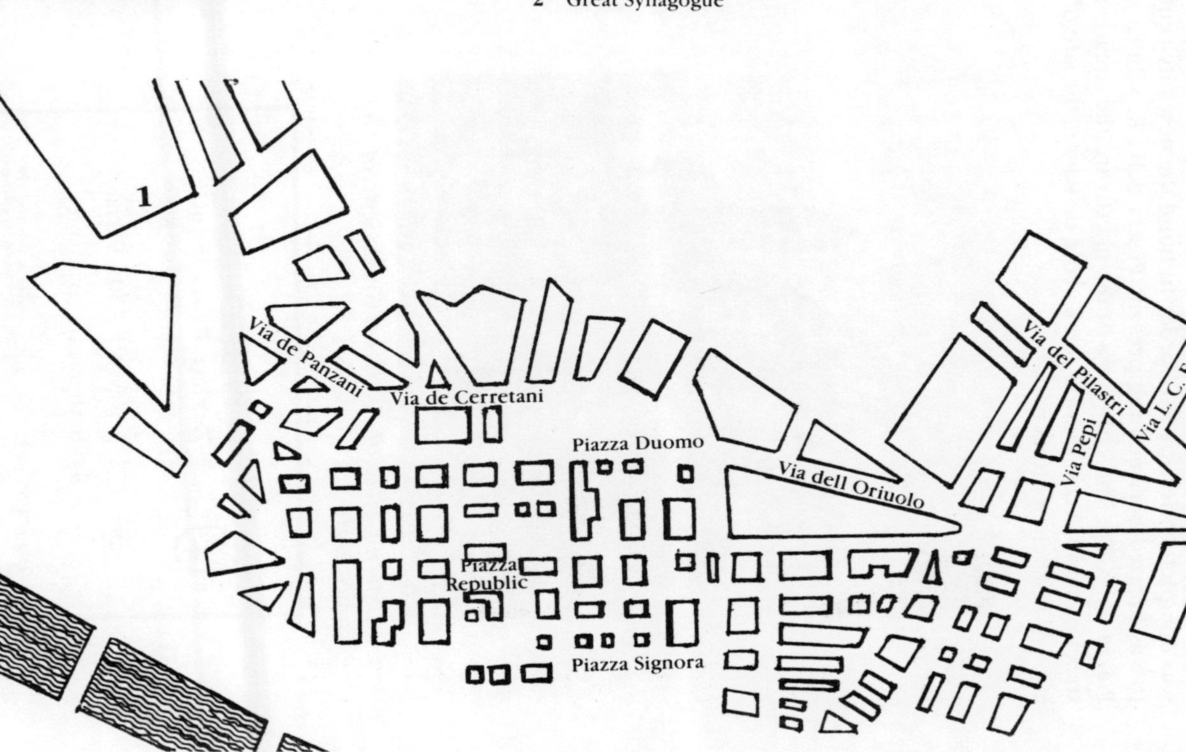
1 Railroad Station
2 Great Synagogue
1
2
Via de Panzani
Via de Cerretani
Piazza Duomo
Via dell Oriuolo
Via del Pilastri
Via Pepi
Via L. C. Farini
Piazza Republic
Piazza Signora

ence. The ghetto existed from 1570-1848. The site of the ghetto was completely destroyed in order to build the new city-centre. It was located between the present Piazza della Republica and Piazza dell'Olio. The only signs of the ghetto are the square and street names of Via Condotta and Cortile de Bagne, the site of an ancient mikveh or ritual bath.

Exterior view of the Great Synagogue of Florence, Italy.

LEGHORN (LIVORNO)

In 1548, Cosimo I de Medici wanted to develop the cities of Leghorn and Pisa into free trading ports. He issued an invitation to all people, promising amnesties, tax exemptions, freedom of trade and religion. Ferdinand I de Medici extended the invitation further to the Jews of Europe by not compelling them to wear the yellow badges to sermons or forced baptisms, but permitting the construction of synagogues and granting the Jews Tuscan citizenship. Thousands of Jews came, especially from Spain and Portugal, and created what was to be known as the "Jerusalem of Italy." Leghorn never had a ghetto. The Jews lived in a quarter in the center of the city, free from all regulations. There was great cultural development. At one time there were six theological academies and schools for humanist studies. Sir Moses Montefiore was born in Leghorn on October 24, 1874, while his parents were on a visit from England.

The Great Synagogue of 1602 was said to have been the finest in Italy. It was destroyed by Allied bombings, during raids on the ports, during World War II.

SYNAGOGUE Via del Tempio 3

The new synagogue was built in 1962 on the site of the original 1602 building. It is an extremely modern structure. Designed by architect di Castro, the shape of the building symbolizing the crown of the Torah. The interior is designed in an elliptical shape, with the seating following the Spanish (Sephardic) ritual. The ark was taken from the 17th century synagogue of Pesaro, Italy. Its Baroque design utilizes gilded floral patterns and a crown of the Torah.

The basement of the synagogue houses an ark and bimah from the 17th century Spanish synagogue at Ferrara. The ark of the Oratory of Via Micali, which is gilded and topped by three quadrangular domes, is said to have been brought by Portuguese Jewish exiles who flooded into Leghorn in the 15th century.

The ark in the Leghorn Synagogue was removed from a 17th century synagogue in Pesaro. Italy.

TURIN

MOLE ANTONELLIANA
Via Montebello + Via Giuseppi Verdi

The Jewish community of Turin decided to build a synagogue in

TURIN

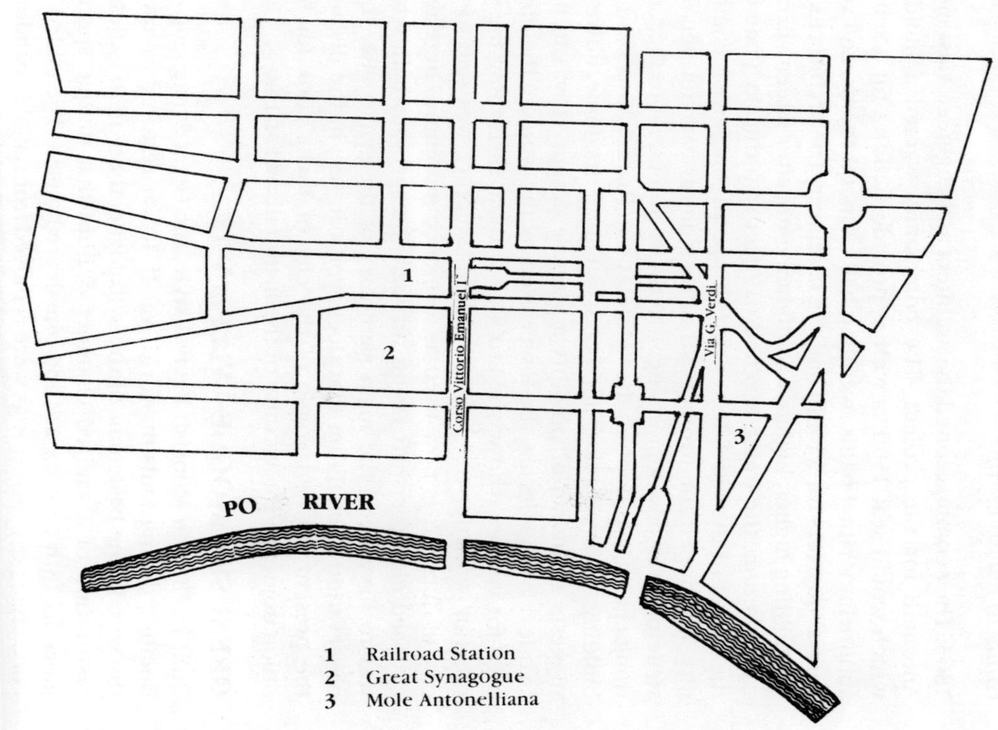
Corso Vittorio Emanuel I°
Via G. Verdi
1
2
3
PO RIVER
1 Railroad Station
2 Great Synagogue
3 Mole Antonelliana

1863. They commissioned the architect and engineer Alessandro Antonelli for the project. The community wanted a building which would seat 1500 as well as provide facilities for a school auditorium, ritual baths, wedding halls, funeral rooms, and residential quarters for a rabbi and the caretaker. The architect kept on building higher, higher, and higher, until, after fifteen years of construction, the frame reached 619 feet into the sky (one half the height of the Eiffel Tower). At this point, the Jewish community abandoned the project. All of their funds had run out. The structure was now a monument to the architect, more than anything else. It was dubbed the "Mole Antonelliana." At its base the building followed a simplified classical motif. Its dome, however, suggests an Indian or possibly a Siamese design. It was to have two levels of galleries: the lower used by the women, the upper used for visitors who wished to look without disturbing the services or worshippers. The unfinished structure was sold to the city of Turin. It is now used as a science museum. There is an exposed elevator shaft rising through the spacious hall, which was to have been the main sanctuary of the synagogue, to an observation deck. From that deck, you can see, in the distance, the present day synagogue of the city of Turin. Look for four onion domes in the vicinity of the main railroad station.

GREAT SYNAGOGUE Via Pia V 12

Built in 1884 in Moorish Revival style, the Great Synagogue was bombed during raids in World War II. It was restored following the war. In the basement of the synagogue, there is an exquisite restoration of a vaulted chamber. Within that unique space, a glorious 18th century ark and bimah are housed. The gilded Rococo style holy furnishings were removed from an old abandoned synagogue from the nearby village of Chieri. The bimah is an octagonal structure raised on two steps. An open canopy of scrolls crowns the eight twisted columns. The concept of this bimah is basically that of the Baldachino, the imposing tabernacle by Bernini, which encloses the Altar of St. Peter's in Rome. It is said that the columns of the Holy Temple in Jerusalem were designed as spiral shafts. Note: There is is similar ark and bimah

The Mole Antonelliana in Turin, Italy, was originally designed as a synagogue.

located in the old synagogue in Carmagnola. Since there is no longer an active Jewish community in that village, the synagogue is now closed.

NOTE: There are several closed-down synagogues throughout Italy which have shipped their arks and bimahs to Israel. Below is a partial list of the Italian towns from which arks or bimahs were shipped, along with the Israeli recipients of these treasures.

Busito *Talbiah, Jerusalem*
Conegliano *Tempio Italiano, Jerusalem*
Corregio *Hapoel Hamizrachi Synagogue, Jerusalem*
Mantua *Beit Yeshayahu Synagogue, Tel Aviv*
Mantua *Ponovitzer Yeshiva, Bnei Brak*
Padua *Yad Eliyahu*
Padua *Hechal Shlomo, Jerusalem*
Pesaro *Yochanan bin Zakai Synagogue, Jerusalem*
Reggio Emilia *Kiryat Shmuel*
Vittorio Venneto *Israel Museum, Jerusalem*

SYNAGOGUES

Alessandria *Via Milano 5 #62-224*

Ancona *Via Astagno #22-905*

Asti *Via Ottolenghi 4*

Bologna *Via Marco Finzi #232-066*

Casale Monferrato *Vicolo Salmone Olper 44 #71-807*

Ferrara *Via Mazini 95 #47-004, #34-240*

Florence *Via L.C. Farini 4 #210-763, #212-549*

Genoa *Via Bertora 6 #891-513*

Gorizia *Via Ascoli 13*

Leghorn *Via del Tempio 3 #24-290, #810-265*

Mantua *Via G.Govi 11 #321-490*

Merano *Via Schiller 14 #23-127*

Milan Tempio Centrale *Via Guastalla 19 #808-947*
Ohel Jaakov *Via Cellini 2 #708-877*
Beth Shlomo *Corso di Porta Romana 3*
Oratorio di Via Jommelli 18 #236-504

Oratorio della Scuola *Via Sally Mayer 4/6*
Oratorio Sefardita *Via delle Tuberose 14 #41-51-660*
Oratorio di Via Eupili 8
Oratorio Nouvo Residenza per Anziani *Via Leone XII #1*

Modena *Piazza Mazzini 26 #223-978*

Napoli *Via Cappella Vecchia 31 #416-386*

Padua *Via San Martino e Solferino 13 #23-524*

Parma *Vicolo Cervi 4*

Pisa *Via Palestro 24 #27-269*

Rome Tempio Maggiore *Lungotevere Cenci 9 #65-64-648*
Tempio Spagnolo *Via Catalana*
Oratorio di Castro *Via Balboa 33 #47-59-881*
Via della Borgata della Magliana #52-32-634
Lungotevere Sanzio 12
Via Garefagnana 4 #42-44-521

Turin *Via S.Pio V 12 #65-08-332*

Trieste *Via Donizetti 2 #768-17*

Venice *Ghetto Vecchio 1188a #715-012*

Vercelli *Via Foa*

Verona *Via Rita Rosani #21-112*

Viareggio *Via del Oleadri*

MIKVEHS

Ancona *Via Astagno #55-654*

Bologna *Via Gombruti 9 #232-066*

Ferrara *Via Saraceno 106/a + Via Carmelino #33-996*

Florence *Via L.C.Farini 4 #210-763, #212-549*

Milan *Via Guastalla 19 #808-947*

Rome *Lungotevere Cenci + Via Balboa 33 #65-64-648*

Venice *(Jewish Rest Home) Ghetto Nuovo 2874 #716-002*

KOSHER HOTELS

Milan-Marittima (Ravenna) *Adriatic Riviera #991-281*

Riccione Hotel Lido Mediterranea *(kosher food available during the summer only)*

Rimini Grand Hotel *(kosher food available during the summer only)* Tel. 0541/24211 Telex. 550022 GRANDH

Rome Hotel Carmel *Via Goffredo Mameli 11 #580-9921*

Viareggio *Principe di Piemonte*

KOSHER RESTAURANTS & PROVISIONS

Bologna *(Lubavitch) Via Dagnini 24*
Menza *Via Gonbruti 9 #232-066, #340-936*

Ferrara *(butcher) Via Saraceno 106a #33-996*

Florence il Cuscussu *Via Farini 2a #241890*
(butcher) Via del Macci 106 #666-534
(butcher) #666-549

Genoa *(butcher) Via s.Zita 44r #586-573*
(grocer) Corso Torino 2r #587-658

Leghorn *(butcher) Mercata Centrale #39-474*

Milan Eshel Israel *Via Benvenuto Cellini 2 #708-877. (Open 12 noon to 3.00 p.m. and 7.00 p.m. to 9.30 p.m.)*
(butcher) Via Cesare da Sesto 7 #83-51-011
(butcher) Via S.Maurillo 3 #878-834
(butcher) Piazza Pio XI 5 #873-089
(grocer) Via Montecuccoli 21 #415-98-35
(butcher) Viale Ranzoni 7 #404-2977

Modena *(grocer)* Macelleria Duomo *stand #5, Mercato Coperto*

Rome Pensione Carmel *Via G.Mameli 11 #580-9921*
(grocer) Via Portico d'Ottavia 1b #65-41-364
(butcher) Via Filipo Turati 110 #733-358
(butcher) Piazza Bologna 11 #429-120
(butcher) Via Urbana 117 #487-743
(butcher) Via Livorno 16 #426-408
(Lubavitch) Rabbi Hazan *Via Lorenzo il Magnifico 23 #424-6962*

Turin *(butcher) Via XX Settembre 2 #543-312*

Venice *(Jewish Rest Home) la Casa di Riposo #716-002*
(grocer) S.Luca 4578 #24-658

Viareggio *(butcher) Piazza del Mercato Nuovo #42-691 (summer only)*

AMERICAN EXPRESS OFFICES

Bari *Via Melo 168 #21-35-08*

Bologna *Piazza XX Settembre 6 #26-47-24*

Cagliari *Piazza Deffenn 14 #65-29-71*

Catania (Sicily) *Via Etnea 65 #31-61-55*

Florence *Via Degli Speziali 7/r #217-241*

Genoa *Via Ettore Vernazza 48 #59-55-51*

Milan *19 Via Vittor Pisani #670-9060*

Naples *Via S.Brigada 68 #36-03-77*

Padua *Via Risorgimento 20 #66-61-33*

Palermo *Via Emerico Amari 38 #587-144*

Rome *Piazza di Spagna 38 #6764*

Trieste *Piazza Unita d'Italia 6 #62621*

Turin *Via Accademia delle Science 1 #51-38-41*

Venice *1471 San Moise (San Marco) #700-844*

Verona *Galleria Pellicciai 13 #594-988*

YOUTH HOSTELS

Brindisi *Via Nicola Broad 2 #222-126*

Como *Via Bellinzona 2 #558-722*

Ferrara *Via Bennenuto Tisi da Garofalo 5 #21098*

Florence *Via Augusto Righi 2 #601-451*

Genoa *Via Cinque Maggio 79 #387-370*

Mantova Sparafucile *Strada Legnaghese #322-415*

Milan *Via Martino Bassi 2 #367-095*

Naples *Salita della Grotta a Piedrigrotta 23 #685-346*

Pesaro Ardizio *Strada Panoramica dell'Ardizio #55798*

Ravenna *Via Aurelio Nicolodi 12 #420-405*

Roma *Viale delle Olimpiadi 61 #396-4709*

Siena *Via Fiorentina #52212*

Trieste *Viale Miramare 331 #224-102*

Venice *Fondamenta Zitelle 86 (Giudecca) #38211*

Verona *Salita Fontana del Ferro 15 #590-360*

RAILROAD TIMETABLES

Milan to:

Destination	Times
Amsterdam	7.10—22.28
Barcelona	6.40—21.21
Brussels	17.55—7.37
Copenhagen	9.20—6.45
Frankfurt	7.10—16.17
London	19.05—13.37
Nice	13.10—19.18
Paris	8.52—16.23
Rome	13.00—20.07
Venice	9.05—12.24
Vienna	9.35—22.20
Zurich	9.10—13.50

Germany

The first Jews to reach Germany were merchants who went there in the wake of the Roman legions and settled in the Roman-founded Rhine towns. The earliest detailed record of a Jewish community in Germany, referring to Cologne, is found in imperial decrees issued in 321. There was no continuous Jewish settlement in Germany until the 10th century. Jewish traders from Italy and France settled in Speyer, Worms, and Mainz. These three cities, known as "*Shum*"(an abbreviation based on the initial letters of the Hebrew names of the cities), were to become great centers for Jewish education. Among the many noted rabbis of this "Jerusalem of Germany" were Rabbi Gershom ben Judah (known as the "Light of the Diaspora," *Me'or ha Golah*), who established a seminary for Talmudic studies in Mainz around the year 1000, and one of his disciples, Rabbi Shlomo Yitzchaki (commonly referred to as Rashi), who lived in Troyes, France, but attended the yeshiva in Worms, Germany.

For three centuries, the Jewish communities of Germany prospered. In 1096, the First Crusade began. It heralded the process of disintegration which gathered momentum throughout the Middle Ages. Before long, it lead to the persecution of the Jews, which has continued ever since, century after century, in the form of blood libels and burnings at the stake. The Jews were never expelled from the whole of Germany (as in France, Spain, and Portugal) since it was not yet united. The Jews would move to another "land," sometimes only a few miles away, which offered them a temporary haven. Nevertheless, many thousands of

WEST GERMANY

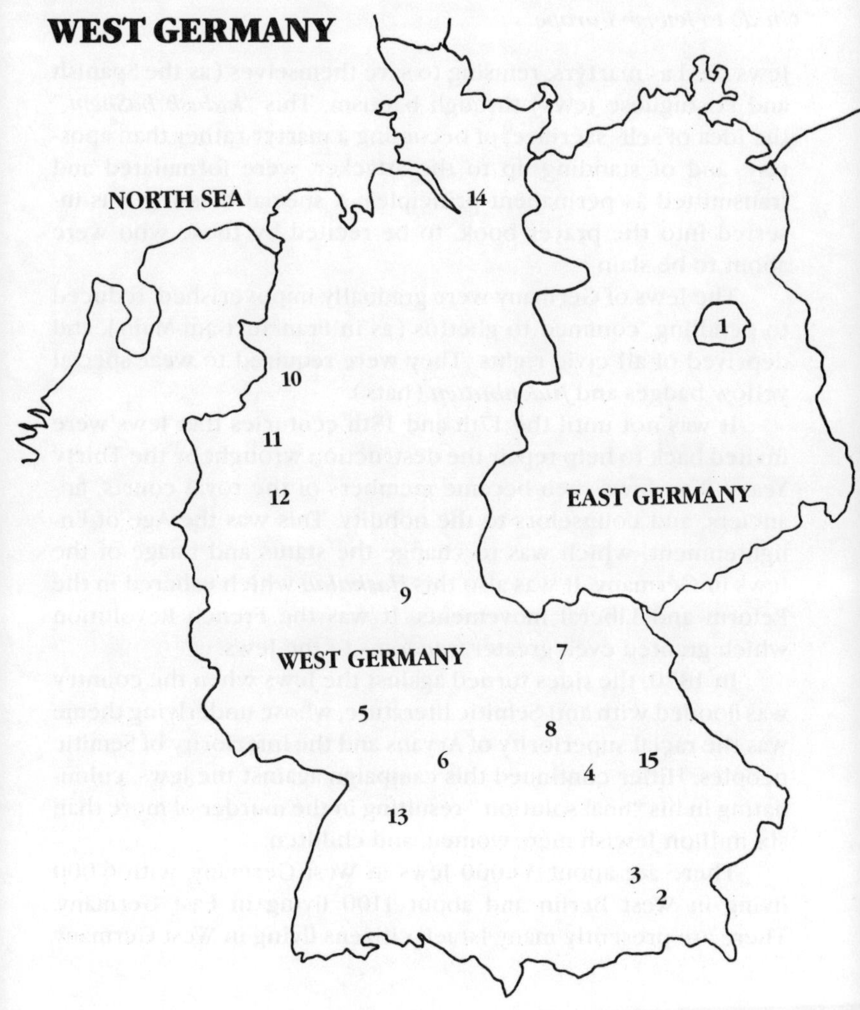

1 Berlin
2 Munich
3 Dachau
4 Ansbach
5 Worms
6 Schwäbisch Hall
7 Bamberg
8 Rothenburg
9 Frankfurt-am-Main
10 Essen
11 Cologne
12 Bonn
13 Stuttgart
14 Hamburg
15 Nuremberg

Jews died as martyrs, refusing to save themselves (as the Spanish and Portuguese Jews) through baptism. This "*kidush haShem*," the idea of self- sacrifice, of becoming a martyr rather than apostasy, and of standing up to the attacker, were formulated and transmitted as permanent principles. A special blessing was inserted into the prayer book, to be recited by those who were about to be slain.

The Jews of Germany were gradually impoverished, reduced to peddling, confined to ghettos (as in Frankfurt-am-Main), and deprived of all civic rights. They were required to wear special yellow badges and *Judenhutten* (hats).

It was not until the 17th and 18th centuries that Jews were invited back to help repair the destruction wrought by the Thirty Years' War. Jews then became members of the royal courts, financiers, and counselors to the nobility. This was the Age of Enlightenment, which was to change the status and image of the Jews in Germany. It was also this *Haskalah* which ushered in the Reform and Liberal movements. It was the French Revolution which granted even greater freedoms to the Jews.

In 1870, the tides turned against the Jews when the country was flooded with anti-Semitic literature, whose underlying theme was the racial superiority of Aryans and the inferiority of Semitic peoples. Hitler continued this campaign against the Jews, culminating in his "final solution," resulting in the murder of more than six million Jewish men, women, and children.

There are about 34,000 Jews in West Germany, with 6,000 living in West Berlin and about 1100 living in East Germany. There are presently many Israeli citizens living in West Germany.

ANSBACH

ANSBACH SYNAGOGUE

Located in the old medieval section of the town, the Ansbach

Synagogue was built in 1746 by the court Jews who owed their loyalty to the Margrave Carl Wilhelm Frederick. He commissioned an Italian architect, Leopold Retti, who designed it in the Italian Baroque style. The Jews were well-liked by all the local citizens. It was because of this benevolence that the synagogue was spared from destruction.

The interior of the ancient synagogue of Ansbach, Germany.

On November 9, 1938, the Nazis burned down hundreds of synagogues throughout Germany as a reprisal for the killing of a German diplomat in Paris. Thousands of Jews were arrested and the windows of Jewish stores were shattered, hence the name, "Night of the Broken Glass" or *Kristallnacht*, in German. When the Gestapo approached the synagogue in Ansbach, the mayor of the town refused to obey the order to burn down the synagogue.

He rather took some wet rags, placed them inside the synagogue, and ignited them. There was much smoke but no real fire. The Gestapo was convinced that the synagogue was actually burning, and did not interfere with the "fire." A non-Jewish neighbor saw the smoke emanating from the synagogue, quickly ran inside and rescued the Torahs. She hid them near her house and didn't tell anyone where they were located. She died during the war and took her secret with her. To this day, nobody knows where the ancient Torahs are located!

The Ansbach Synagogue is the only Jewish house of worship in all of Germany which has survived intact. There are no Jews living in Ansbach today. The old synagogue has been restored and is now a museum. It can be visited by contacting Mr.Adolphe Lang, the town archivist in the Ratthaus.

NOTE: There is an old Jewish cemetery in the neighboring village of Bechofen which dates back to the 18th century.

EAST BERLIN

Crossing into Communist East Berlin is not that difficult. You do not need a formal photographed visa. All you must have in order to receive a 12-hour visa is a valid passport and about $20 which you must change into East German currency. Be prepared to spend some time waiting in the customs office.

ORANIENBURGERSTRASSE SYNAGOGUE REMAINS 30 Oranienburgerstrasse (East Berlin)

This temple was designed in 1859 by Eduard Knoblauch and August Stueler and was completed in 1866. It was designed in

Moorish and Gothic forms and combined the use of polychrome brick and cast iron. This was the largest synagogue in Germany, with a seating capacity of 3,200. Adjoining the synagogue, on the right, is the present day Jewish community center. On the left, was a Jewish hospital and Jewish museum. On November 9, 1938, the Nazis set fire to the synagogue. The adjoining buildings housed German (non-Jewish) citizens, who persuaded the Gestapo to extinguish the fire in the synagogue since it would next burn down their houses. The Nazis did put out the flames, only after all of the interior of the synagogue was totally gutted. To this day, the skeletal shell of the synagogue remains. There are still some original Hebrew entablatures on the facade.

The ruins of the magnificent Oranienburgerstrasse Synagogue in East Berlin.

JEWISH CEMETERY 2 Lothringerstrasse (in the Weissensea section—East Berlin)

The *Judische Friedhof,* Jewish cemetery, is the newest and largest in Germany, containing more than 115,000 graves. The cemetery was restored and reconstructed after World War II. Among the black granite mausoleums, are the great personalities in German-Jewish history between 1880 and 1939. The orthodox section, known as the Adath Israel Cemetery, has not been restored. Many of the tombstones are still knocked-over, many are missing, and wild grass abounds.

All that remains of the Fasanenstrasse Synagogue in West Berlin is the limestone portal.

WEST BERLIN

JEWISH COMMUNITY CENTER 80 Fasanenstrasse

Located near the Kurfurstendam, the Jewish Community Center was built on the site of Berlin's most fashionable synagogue, the Fasanenstrasse Temple. The temple was built in 1912 by architect Ehrenfried Hessel in the Romanesque Revival style. Its dominant feature was its three-domed roof. The wedding chamber, in the basement, was decorated with tiles from the Imperial factory, a gift from the Kaiser, who had taken a personal interest in the building of the temple. The temple was totally destroyed during the Kristallnacht. All that remains is the front limestone portal, which has been placed in sharp contrast, at the entrance of the new and modern community center. The community center was designed in 1959 by D.Knoblauch and H.Heise. The community center houses a large auditorium which is used as a synagogue on the High Holy Days, a kosher restaurant, a library, recreation rooms, and religious school classrooms. There are now armed guards stationed behind bullet-proof glass at the reception area. There have been terrorist attacks against the community center several years ago. There are presently about 6,000 Jews living in West Berlin.

COLOGNE

ROONSTRAASE SYNAGOGUE 50 Roonstrasse

Many of the synagogues in Germany at the turn of the century reflected the designs found in the great cathedrals of that country. The Roonstrasse Synagogue was built in 1899 by Emil Schreiterer in the Romanesque Revival style. The building was gutted on the Kristallnacht. It was not until 1957 when a small group of survivors of the Holocaust decided to rebuild. They commissioned Helmut Goldschmidt to redesign the existing structure. He divided the original hall of worship into two parts, horizontally, by putting in a floor at the gallery level. The domed part of the original structure thus became the main synagogue. Below the main synagogue is the social hall. The ground floor contains offices, a room for youth activities, a mikveh, a weekday chapel, Jewish museum, and kosher restaurant.

DACHAU CONCENTRATION CAMP

The first of Hitler's concentration camps, was established in Dachau, a suburban town, near Munich. This concentration camp was constructed to house "political" prisoners, and was actually the prototype for all of Hitler's death camps. The guard towers, electric barbed-wire fences, and moat are still extant. Some of the torture rooms have been converted into a museum, where there are preserved many articles used in daily life by the prisoners, torture instruments, and photographs of crematorium operations. The crematoria are located just left of the massive Jewish memorial and the "grave of thousands of unknown." All of the prison barracks, except one, have been torn down, but their site has been marked by concrete blocks and numbered gravel beds. It is estimated that 207,000 prisoners passed through Dachau, and some 27,000 are known to have been killed there. The railroad tracks, which had a spur right through the center of the town of Dachau, are now being torn up and are being replaced with a bicycle path.

To get to the KZ—Gedankstaat, Concentration Camp Memorial, which is open every day from 9.00 a.m. to 6.00 p.m., take the S-2 Bahn (subway) from the main railroad station in Munich. Get off at the station called "Dachau." Go downstairs, turn left and take bus L-3 to Dachau Ost. Ask the bus driver to let you off at the KZ—Gedankstaat.

The remains of Dachau concentration camp.

ESSEN

STEELERSTRASSE SYNAGOGUE 29 Steelerstrasse

The Essen Synagogue was approached from a forecourt, which

was flanked by covered passages. The architect, Edmund Korner, was inspired by descriptions of the courts of the Temple of Jerusalem, which were closed by stoas. The architect intended that the worshipper should be touched by his subtle theatrical sense as he passed from the narrow entrance under the Neo- Romanesque facade, across the forecourt, and up a broader flight of steps through the spacious lobby and into the vast ever-broadening hall of worship.

The main sanctuary, which seated 1400 persons, was softly radiant with the light diffused through the stained-glass windows and reflected by glass mosaic tiles. Behind the ark were arranged the weekday chapel, meeting hall, library, ritual bath, offices, classrooms, and caretaker's and rabbi's living quarters.

On Kristallnacht, the Nazis attempted to dynamite the building but found it too costly and too structurally sound. The interior was nevertheless gutted. The building now contains a Museum of the Holocaust.

FRANKFURT-AM-MAIN

WESTEND SYNAGOGUE

Designed in 1910 by Franz Roeckle, the Westend Synagogue has a central plan with a domed hall. The Nazis had planned to establish a permanent museum to house Jewish religious treasures taken from destroyed Jewish communities throughout Europe. A similar plan was actually carried out in Prague, Czechoslovakia. The synagogue was therefore spared from destruction. The building was restored by the German government in 1950.

SCHWÄBISCH HALL

In the 17th century, there were itinerant artists who were commissioned to paint the walls and ceilings of wooden (*stahl* or barn) synagogues throughout Poland and Germany. The old wooden synagogue of Bechofen, Germany, was decorated by Eliezer Sussman, an itinerant artist from Poland. That synagogue was set ablaze during Kristallnacht by the well- respected town-physician. Other works by Eliezer Sussman have, however, been preserved. The wall and ceiling paintings of the synagogue in the village of Unterlimpurg, where Jews had been expelled to from the town of Schwäbisch Hall, are now preserved in the Keckenburg Museum of Schwäbisch Hall. The interior of the synagogue room was commissioned in 1739. Eliezer Sussman used polychrome panels, depicting symbolic beasts in medallions against a floral background, as well as a representation of Jerusalem and Hebrew texts. The women's section was behind a wooden screen with peepholes, which the artist contrived to incorporate in his decorative scheme. The Keckenburg Museum is open daily (except Monday) from 9.00 a.m. to 12 noon and from 2.00 p.m. to 5.00 p.m .

Other works by Eliezer Sussman have been preserved and shipped to Israel. The remnants of a 13th century synagogue from Bamberg, which were incorporated into a church during the 1349 massacres, were recently shipped to the Israel Museum, in Jerusalem.

The exquisite wooden ceiling of the small synagogue at Horb, Germany, commissioned by Sussman in 1739, is now on permanent display in the Beit Hatefutsot, Museum of the Diaspora, in Tel Aviv University.

WORMS

RASHI SYNAGOGUE

The original synagogue of Worms was built in 1034 on Judengasse. It was rebuilt in 1175, in the Gothic style. Later additions to the synagogue include a Frauenschul, women's section, in 1213, and the famous yeshiva, known as the Rashi Chapel, in 1624. Rashi, the noted rabbi who wrote commentaries on the Bible and the Talmud, was born in 1040, lived, worked, and died in 1105 in the city of Troyes, France. He attended the rabbinical academy of Rabbenu Gershom in Worms only for a few years of his life, nevertheless, the city of Worms has adopted Rashi as its son. There is a Rashi House, Rashi Synagogue, and Rashi *Tor*, a gate along the ancient city walls.

There are several legends associated with Rashi's parents. A legend tells that his father cast a precious gem into the sea, rather than surrender it to Christians who desired it for idolatrous purposes. A heavenly voice then foretold the birth of a son who would enlighten the world with his wisdom. Another legend tells of Rashi's mother being imperilled in a narrow street during her pregnancy. She pressed against a wall which formed a niche to rescue her. There is today a niche on the outside wall (in the alleyway), behind the Rashi Synagogue in Worms.

The Rashi Synagogue was totally destroyed during World War II. The present structure is a reconstruction, which was completed in 1961.

In the courtyard, behind the Rashi Chapel, is the original subterranean mikveh (ritual bath), which was built in 1186. It was not destroyed during the war. There is still a natural spring which has supplied water for this mikveh since its original consecration. Chassidim from all parts of the world, come and immerse themselves in this mikveh before Rosh Hashanah.

Today, there are no Jews living in Worms. The Rashi Synagogue is open to the public and guided tours are provided daily from 9.00 a.m to 12 noon and from 2.00 p.m. to 5.00 p.m.

WORMS

1 Railroad Station
2 Rashi Synagogue
3 Judengasse
4 Rashi House
5 Rashi Gate (Tor)
6 Jewish Cemetery
7 Tomb of Rabbi Meir of Rothenberg
8 *Rabbintal*—Valley of the Rabbis
9 New Cemetery
10 Wall of Broken Tombstones

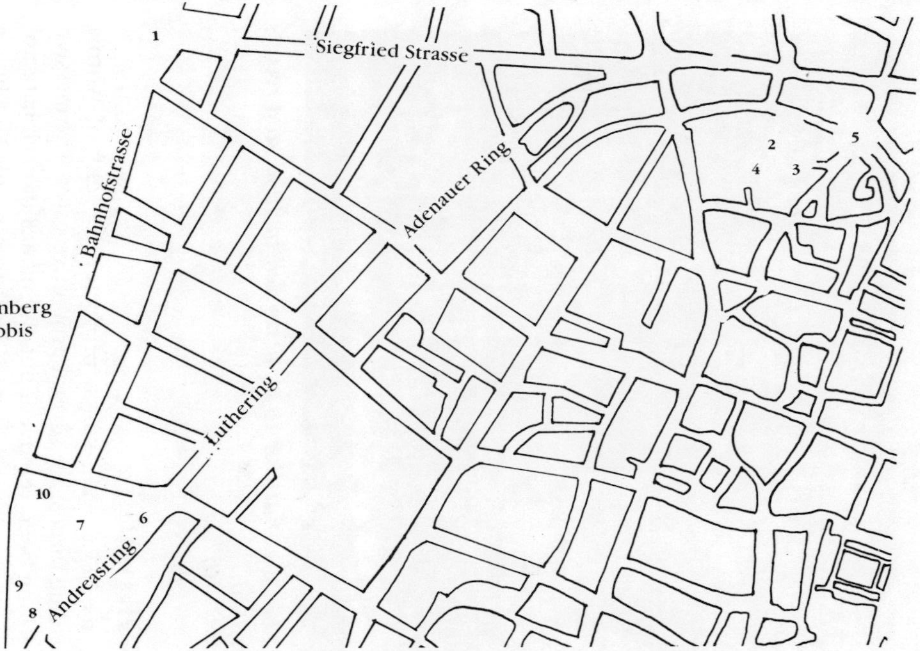

The Rashi Shul was built in 1034, destroyed in 1938, and reconstructed in 1961.

RASHI TOR (GATE)

Along the medieval wall, which protected the city of Worms against invading forces, are several protective gates. The massive doors have long been removed, but the names of each gate are still preserved. At the junction of Judengasse and Karoligner Strasse is the entrance to the old Jewish Quarter. There is a stone marker, engraved in Gothic lettering, indicating that this was the "Raschi Tor."

OLD JEWISH CEMETERY

This is the oldest Jewish cemetery in Europe. The earliest tombstone dates from the year 1076. Many noted rabbis are buried

1 Rome
2 Venice
3 Florence
4 Leghorn
5 Milan
6 Naples
7 Sicily
8 Sardinia
9 Genoa
10 Turin
11 Bologna
12 Brindisi
13 Padua
14 Pisa
15 Como
16 Corsica (French)
17 Elba

1	From Railroad Station	7	Italian Scuola
2	Spanish Scuola	8	Canton Scuola
3	Levantine Scuola	9	Great German Scuola
4	Midrash of Leon de Modena	10	Jewish Rest Home
5	Entrance to the Ghetto Vecchio	11	Holocaust Memorial
6	Ghetto Nuovo	12	Ghetto Nuovissimo

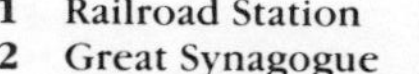

1	Berlin	9	Frankfurt-am-Main
2	Munich	10	Essen
3	Dachau	11	Cologne
4	Ansbach	12	Bonn
5	Worms	13	Stuttgart
6	Schwäbisch Hall	14	Hamburg
7	Bamberg	15	Nuremberg
8	Rothenburg		

The medieval walls surrounding Worms honor the great scholar, Rashi.

here. In 1286, when a great number of Jews wished to emigrate to Palestine, Rabbi Meir of Rothenburg (the Maharam) was taken prisoner. The emperor ordered this imprisonment because he hoped that imprisoning such a respected and prominent rabbi would prevent the Jews from emigrating. He did not want to lose a very reliable source of income, the so-called "Judensteuer," a tax raised from Jews only. Rabbi Meir refused to let the Jewish community of Worms pay the 23,000 marks ransom for his release from prison. Rabbi Meir died in 1293 in Ensishein prison. It was not until 14 years later that the ransom was paid and the remains of Rabbi Meir were released. A rich merchant, Alexander Solomon Wimpfen, paid the high ransom and was honored by being buried next to Rabbi Meir. Since the year 1307, the two of them have rested side by side. There are pebbles and slips of

paper atop each tombstone. The little stones are symbolic of when the Jews buried their dead in the wilderness (for forty years). In an effort to protect the remains from being disinterred by wild animals, they heaped up stones on the graves. Today, the little stones are signs of reverence. The slips of paper have a similar significance. Visitors write personal requests and wishes on them. This custom is also observed at the Wailing Wall, in Jerusalem, where people put prayers on small slips of paper into the crevasses of the Wall. It is a custom that the dead are buried facing Jerusalem. There is no explanation, but all of the thousands of tombstones (except one) in the Worms cemetery are facing due south instead of east, southeast.

In the southern tip of the cemetery, there is a small valley known as the "Rabbinthal" or "Valley of the Rabbis." Well known rabbis of Worms are buried here including: Rabbi Jacob ben

The old Jewish cemetery in Worms is the oldest in Europe.

Moses Moellin (Maharil),died 1427; Rabbi Elijah ben Moses Loanz (Ba'al Shem), died 1636; Rabbi Jair Chaim Bacharach, died 1702, and Rabbi Menachem Mendel Rothschild, died 1732. Please note that Rashi is not buried in this cemetery. His burial place is not known.

There is a wall on the north side of the cemetery, which contains fragments of tombstones. These are remains of destroyed and desecrated tombstones, which were used during the massacres of the Black Plague (1349) to construct roads and houses.

The higher level of the cemetery is the recent section. The tombstones are engraved in both Hebrew and German, a sign of the assimilation process during the 19th and 20th centuries. The Nazis did not touch this cemetery during the war. It was because of the chief archivist of Worms, Dr.F.M.Ilbert, who showed the sites of Worms to the SS-leader, Himmler, when Himmler visited the city. Himmler found the cemetery very interesting. When the Nazis decided to erect buildings on the cemetery, Dr.Ilbert argued that Himmler had a very special interest in the preservation of the Jewish cemetery. Ilbert recommended that the builders ask Berlin for permission before beginning to level the cemetery. Obviously, no one dared to make inquiries in Berlin concerning this matter. That way Dr. Ilbert succeeded in blocking the plans of the Nazis. Moreover, he preserved the records and documents of the Jewish community, including the two volumes of the Worms *machzor*, dating from the 13th century. Much of this material has been sent to Israel.

SYNAGOGUES

Aachen *Oppenhoffalee 50 #50-16-90*

Amberg *Salzgasse 5 #13140*

Augsburg *Halderstr. 8 #51-79-85*

Bad Homburg *Holderlinweg 28 #3740*

Bad Kreuznach *Gymnasialstr. 11 #26991*

Bad Nauheim *Karlstr. 34 #5605*

Bamberg *Willy-Lessingstr. 7 #2-32-67*

Bayreuth *Munzgasse 2 #65407*

Bielefeld *Stapenhorststr. 35 #12-37-52*

Bonn *Templstr. 2 #21-35-60*

Baden-Baden *Werderstr. 2 #22142*

Braunschweig *Steinstr. 4 #22417*

Bremen *Schwachhauser Heerstr. 117 #49-51-04*

Celle *Brunkhorststr. 48*

Coblenz *Schlachthofstr. 5 #42223*

Cologne *Roonstr. 50 #23-56-26*

Darmstadt *Osannstr. 11 #48719*

Detmold *Allee 13 #22839*

Dortmund *Prinz Friedrich Karlstr. 9 #52-84-97*

Düsseldorf *Zeitenstr. 50 #48-03-13*

Essen *Sedanstr. 46 #27-34-13*

Frankfurt-am-Main *Baumweg 5 #29-46-92*
Freherr-vom-Steinstr. 30 #72-62-63
Roderberweg 29 #61-59-14

Freiburg *Holbeinstr. 25 #74-223*

Fulda *Buttlarstr 14b #70252*

Fürth *Julienstr 2 #77-08-79*

Gelsenkirchen *Von-der-Reckestr. 9 #20-66-28*

Giessen *Nordanlage 7 #31162*

Hagen *Potthofstr. 16 #13289*

Hamburg *Hohe Weide 34 #49-29-04*

Hanover *Haeckelstr. 10 #81-27-62*

Heidelberg *Rohrbacher Str. 18 #20820*

Herford *Riegelkamp 8b #72739*

Lübeck *St. Annen Str. 13 #76650*

Kaiserlautern *Basteigasse 4 #69720*

Karlsruhe *Kneilinger Allee 11 #72036*

Kassel *Bremerstr.9 #12960*

Krefeld *Wiederstr. 17b #20648*

Mainz *Forsterstr. 2 #63990*

Mannheim *Maximilianstr. 6 #441295*

Marburg/Lahn *Alter Kirchhainer Weg 1 #23228*

Minden *Kampstr. 6 #23437*

Monchengladbach-Rheydt *Albertusstr. 54 #23879*

Mülheim *Kampstr. 7 #35191*

Munich *Possarstr. 15 #26-39-88*
Reichenbachstr. 27 #201-49-60
Schulstr. 30
Georgenstr. 71

Münster *Klosterstr. 6 #44909*

Neustadt *Hauber Allee 13 #2652*

Nuremberg *Wielandstr. 6 #331888*

Offenbach *Kaiserstr. 109 #814874*

Paderborn *Pipinstr. 32 #22596*

Passau *Brunngasse 2*

Recklinghausen *Am Polizeiprasidium 3 #24525*

Regensburg *Am Brixener Hof 2 #562600*

Saarbrücken *Lortzingstr. 8 #35152*

Straubing *Wittlebacherstr. 2 #1387*

Stuttgart *Hospitalstr. 36 #29-56-65*

Trier *Kaiserstr. 25 #41096*

Weiden *Ringstr. 17 #32794*

Wiesbaden *Friedrichstr. 33 #30-18-70*

Wuppertal *Friedrich-Ebert-Str. 73 #30-02-33*

Wurzburg *Valentin-Beckerstr. 11 #51190*

West Berlin *(Liberal) Pestalozzistr. 14 #313-84-11*
Dernbergstr. 26 #321-20-56
Frankelufer 10 #614-51-31
Joachimstaler Str. 13 #881-30-31
Fasaenstr 79 #881-35-38

East Berlin *Rykestr. 53 #448-52-98*
Oranienburgerstr. 28 #282-33-27

MIKVEHS

Munich *Possartstr. 15 #26-39-88*
Reichenbachstr. 27 #201-49-60

Würzburg *Valentin Becker Str. 11 #5-11-90*

KOSHER RESTAURANTS

Bad Nauheim Hotel Acadia *Lindenstr. 15 #3906*

Berlin (East) *(butcher) Eberswalder Str. 20 #448-22-84*

Berlin (West) *Fasanestr. 79 #881-35-38*
Schalom Snack Bar *Wielandstr. 43 #312-11-31*

Cologne *Roonstr. 50 #23-56-26*

Frankfurt-am-Main *Friedrichstr. 27 #72-86-18 (lunch only)*
Hebelstr. 15 #59-11-23

Stuttgart *Hospitalstr. 36 #29-56-65*

Munich *Rechenbachstr. 27 #201-49-60*

Hamburg *(Lubavitch) Rabbi Kaminker Bogenstr. 27*

AMERICAN EXPRESS OFFICES

Berlin (West) *Kurfuerstendamm #882-7575*

Bremen *Am Wall 138 #314171*

Düsseldorf *Heinrich Heine Allee 14 #80222*

Frankfurt-am-Main *Steinweg 5 #21051*

Hamburg *Kirchenallee 34 #280-1101*

Heidelberg *Friedrich Ebert Anlage 16 #29001*

Munich *Promenadplatz 6 #21990*

Stuttgart *Lautenschlagerstr. 3 #20890*

East Germany

Berlin (East) Reisebuero der DDR. 'Berlin Tourist'
5 Alexanderplatz #2150

YOUTH HOSTELS

Baden-Baden *Hardberstr. 34 #52223*

Berlin (West) *Bayernallee 36 #305-3055*
Hermsdorfer Damm 48 #404-1610
Kluckstr. 3 #261-1097
Badeweg 1 #803-2034

Bonn *Haager Weg 42 #281-200*

Bremen *Kalkstr. 6 #171369*

Darmstadt *Landgraf Georg Str. 119 #45293*

Düsseldorf *Düsseldorfstr. 1 #574-041*

Essen *Pastoratsberg 2 #491163*

Frankfurt-am-Main *Am Deutschherrnufer 12 #619058*

Hamburg *Alfred Wegner Weg 5 #313488*

Hanover *Ferdinand Wilhelm Fricke Weg 1 #322941*

Heidelberg *Tiergartenstr. 5 #42066*

Cologne *An der Schanz 14 #767081*

Mainz *Am Fort Weisenau #85332*

Manheim *Rheinpromenade 21 #822718*

Munich *Winthirplatz 9 #131156*
Miesingerstr. 4 #723-6550

Nuremberg *Kaiserstallung, Burg 2 #221024*

Rothenburg *Rossmuhle #4510*

Schwäbisch Hall *Langenfeldderweg 5 #41050*

Speyer *Am Leinpfad 4 #75380*

Stuttgart *Haussmannstr. 27 #241583*

Trier *Maarstr. 156 #41092*

Worms *Dechaneigasse 1 #25780*

RAILROAD TIMETABLES

Munich to:

Destination	Times
Amsterdam	9.00—20.44
Berlin	7.44—16.48
Copenhagen	9.30—22.50
London	8.43—22.03
Paris	7.19—16.59
Rome	8.20—21.10
Venice	9.44—15.36
Zurich	9.08—13.50

Switzerland

The first mention of Jews living in Switzerland was in Basel, in the year 1213, when it was one of the major Jewish communities in the Holy Roman Empire. Jews migrated to Switzerland from Alsace and southern Germany on the one hand, and from France on the other. The stream of immigration gained in intensity after the expulsion of Jews from France in 1306. The principal occupation of these groups of Jews was moneylending. The life of the Jews until 1348 was relatively free of any major upheavals, with the exception of Bern, where, as a result of a blood libel (ca.1294), some Jews were executed and the rest expelled. The Ogre Fountain in Bern still stands as a bitter reminder of the blood libel—that Jewish "monsters" sacrificed Christian children on Good Friday.

In 1348, the whole of Swiss Jewry was threatened with extermination. The Black Death having reached the countryside around Lake Geneva (Savoy), a number of Jews in the town of Chillon were tortured to confess to having caused the plague by poisoning the wells. As each town throughout Switzerland, and all of Europe, was struck by the plague, the Jews were burnt at the stake.

In 1622, all Jews were banished from Switzerland. Only Jewish physicians were permitted to remain. After 1648, some Jews started moving into the northern canton of Aargau, and lived in the two villages of Lengnau and Endingen. They were not permitted to own land but were permitted to trade, buy, and sell at fairs and markets. Many of the Jews of these two villages were

SWITZERLAND

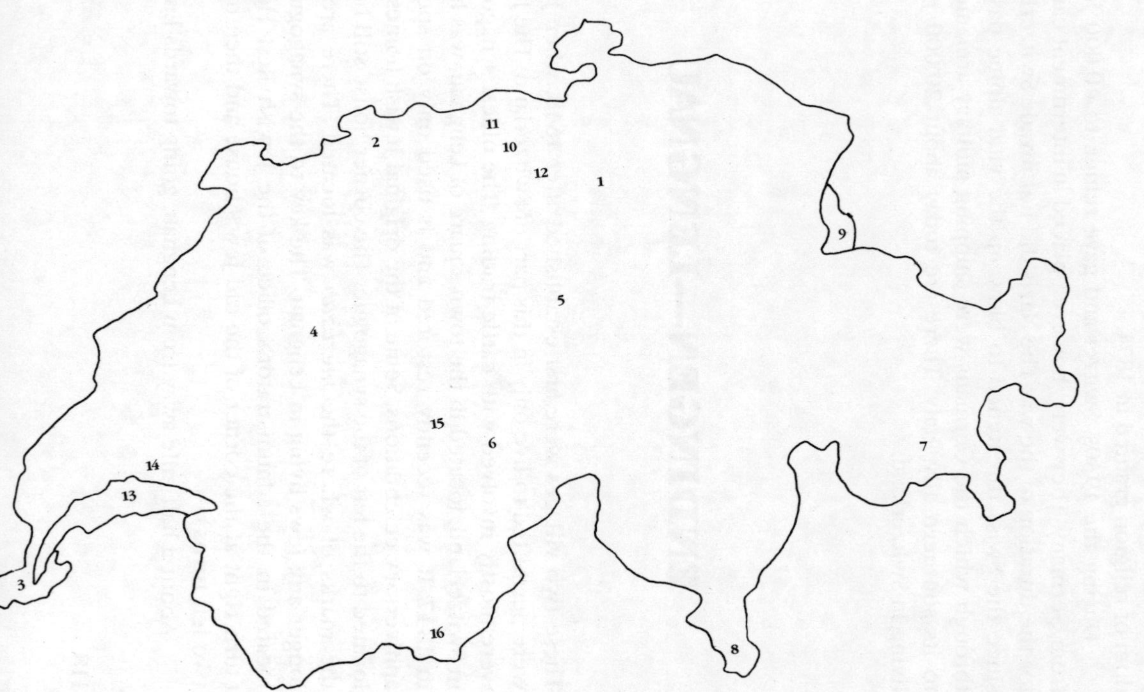

1 Zurich
2 Basel
3 Geneva
4 Bern
5 Luzern
6 Grindelwald
7 St. Moritz
8 Lugano
9 Liechtenstein
10 Lengnau
11 Endingen
12 Baden
13 Lake Geneva
14 Lausanne
15 Interlaken
16 Zermatt

cattle dealers. They were Jewish cowboys.

Influenced by the ideas of the French Revolution, the proclamation of the Helvetian Republic (1798) was a turning point in the history of the Jews of Switzerland. Jews were now granted partial freedom of movement, residence, and trade, with full freedom of religion granted in 1874.

During the 1930s, Switzerland gave refuge to 40,000 Jews from Germany. They were, however, placed in internment camps for the duration of the war.The Nazis did not invade Switzerland since the Swiss threatened to blow up the vital alpine passes, through which the Germans were shipping military armaments to its southern ally, Italy. There are today about 20,000 Jews living in Switzerland.

ENDINGEN—LENGNAU

These two villages were first established after 1648, when Jews were permitted to live only in this part of Switzerland. The Jews were mostly involved with cattle trading. The oldest synagogue in Switzerland, located in the town square of Lengnau, was built in 1847. It was recently restored and is used only on special anniversary celebrations. Some of the original Jewish homes are located to the left of the synagogue. The corner house still bears the marks of where the *mezuzah* was located. There are no longer any Jews living in Lengnau. The key to the synagogue is located in the administrator's office of the Jewish Rest Home (turn right at the corner of the old Jew's house and then make two left turns).

About a half mile away from Lengnau, going towards Endingen, is the old Jewish cemetery. It is recognized by a cluster of trees, on the right side of the road, and is surrounded by a stone wall. During the first years of settlement in Lengnau, the Jews were forbidden to bury their dead in Switzerland. They had to travel north, to the Rhine River, and bury their dead on an island in the middle of the Rhine River, known as *Juden Insle*, Jews' Island.

Continuing northward, you will arrive at Endingen. This was a truly Jewish *shtetl*. There are no churches in this town. The tallest structure in the town is the synagogue, which was built around 1850. It is the only synagogue designed with bells built into its facade. Those bells would toll in times of danger. The bells do still chime, but only on the quarter hour. There are no longer any Jews living in Endingen.

NOTE: There are regularly scheduled trains to the nearby town of Baden. From Baden, take a bus to either Lengnau or Endingen.

The only synagogue in Europe with a belfry is in Endingen.

BASEL

STADTCASINO 14 Steinenberg

This is the building in which Theodor Herzl convened the first World Zionist Congress, in August 1897. This was the launching of the political movement which led to the establishment of the State of Israel in 1948.

SYNAGOGUE 24 Leimenstrasse

The Byzantine Revival structure designed by Hermann Gauss in 1868 originally called for one central dome. In 1891, the building was enlarged and now has two large bulbous domes. There is a kosher restaurant in the adjoining community center.

BERN

OGRE FOUNTAIN (die Kinderfressbrunner)

The Fountain of the Ogre is a bitter reminder of life during the Middle Ages in Switzerland. The Jews were required to wear special clothing. The Jews' hat or *Judenhut* was one such garment. The term *Yehkeh*, is derived from the special jacket or coat which was required to be worn by Jews in certain German towns. In 1294, the Christians of Bern accused the Jews of kidnapping their children, killing them, and using their blood to bake *matzot* for Passover. This blood libel was repeated many times in the Middle Ages, resulting in entire Jewish communities throughout Europe being uprooted and driven out. The Ogre Fountain depicts, very graphically, the Jewish "monster" sacrificing Christian children on Good Friday.

SYNAGOGUES

Arosa *Metropole Hotel #31-10-58*

Baden *Parkstrasse 17*

Basel *Leimenstr. 24 #228-700, 239-850*
Ahornstr. 14
Birmannsgasse 7 #24-77-16
Rudolstrasse 28 #24-28-45

Bern *Kapellenstr. 2 #254992*

Biel *Ruchlisstr. 3*

Bremgarten *Antonigasse 53*

Delemont *rue de Porretruy*

Fribourg *9 avenue de Rome*

Geneva *place de la Synagogue*
2 place des Eaux
54 route de Malagnou

Grindelwald Silberhorn Hotel *#53-28-22*

Kreuzlingen *Hafenstr. 42*
la Chaux de Fonds *-rue de Parc 63 #21447*

Lausanne *avenue Juste Olivier 1*

Locarno Astoria Hotel *#33-67-61*

Lucerne *Bruchstr. 51*
(yeshiva) Brambergstr. 20

Lugano *11 Via Maderno*
Dan Hotel *Via Fontana #541-061*

Montreux *avenue des Alpes 25 #61-58-39*
(yeshiva) Villa Quisisana #61-21-02

St. Gallen *Frngartenstr. 18*

St. Moritz (Bad) Hotel Edelweiss *#35533*

Winterthur *Rosenstr. 5*

Yverdon *26 bis rue Valentin*

Zurich *Freigutstr. 37 #201-67-46*
Erikastr. 8 #35-79-20, #463-79-20
Lowenstr. 10
(Liberal) Fortuna Gasse 15 #825-4830
Anwandstr. 59 #252-90-46

MIKVEHS

Arosa Metropole Hotel *#311-058 (July-August and December-April)*

Davos Etania Hotel *#36318, #55404*

Geneva 54 route de Malagnou #35-65-46

Grindelwald Silberhorn Hotel *#532-822*

Lucerne *Bruchstr. 51 #45-47-50*

St.Moritz Edelweiss Hotel *#35533 (July-August and December-April)*

Zurich *Freigutstr. 37 #201-73-06*
Erikastr. 8 #463-79-25

Lugano *Via Maderno #23-61-34*

KOSHER RESTAURANTS

Arosa Metropole Hotel *#311-058, #242-2540 (July-August and December-April)*

Basel *Leimenstr. 24 #22-87-00, #23-98-50. (Open 11.00 a.m. to 2.00 p.m and 6.30 p.m. to 9.00 p.m. Closed on Wednesday. Arrangements for Sabbath meals must be made in advance.)*

(butcher) Friedrichstr. 26
(butcher) Leimenstr. 41 #23-88-35

Geneva Shalom *78 rue du Rhone #28-90-93*

(Jewish Rest Home 5 rue Cavour #44-87-60

(pizza) 50 route de Malagnou

Grindelwald Silberhorn Hotel *#53-28-22 (December—October.)*

Lausanne *(grocery) 7 avenue Juste Olivier #22-12-65*

Locarno Astoria Hotel *#33-67-61 (April -October)*

Lucerne *(butcher) Bruchtstr. 26 #22-25-60*

Lugano Dan Hotel *Via Fontana #541-061*

Montreux Wajngort *8 rue du Lac #61-25-02*

St. Moritz (Bad) Edelweiss Hotel *#35533 (July-August and December-April)*

Zurich Schalom *Lavaterstr. 33 #201-1476 (During summer this restaurant is open for Sabbath meals, by prior arrangement only.)*
(grocery) Grungasse 2 #241-67-44
(butcher) Lowenstr. 12 #211-52-10
(grocery) Gartenhofstr. 15 #241-22-44
(butcher) Zwinglistr. 17 #242-78-75
(bakery) Waffenplatzstr. 5 #202-30-45
(bakery) Braverstr. 110 #242-87-00
Ben Pitah (pizza) Lavaterstr. 33 (downstairs)

AMERICAN EXPRESS OFFICES

Basel *Aeschengraben 10 #236690*

Bern *Marktgasse 37 #229401*

Geneva *7 rue du Mont Blanc #317600*
13 chemin Louis Dunant #332-550
12 chemin Rieu Florissant #473-277

Lausanne *14 avenue Mon Repos #207-425*

Locarno *Piazza Stazione 2 #336-673*

Lucerne *Schweizerhofquai 4 #501-177*

Lugano *Piazza Manzoni 8 #227-782*

Montreux *avenue des Alpes 43 #624-121*

St.Gallen *Kornhausstr. 15 #208-141*

Zurich *Banhofstr. 20 #211-8370*

YOUTH HOSTELS

Arosa *Hubelstr. #311-397*

Baden *Kanalstr. 7 #261-796*

Basel *St.Alban Kirchrain 10 #230-572*

Bern *Weihergasse 4 #226-316*
la Chaux de Fonds *rue du Doubs 34 #284-315*

Chur *Berggasse 28 #226-563*

Davos *Hohwald #51484*

Fribourg *avenue General Guisan 61 #262-898*

Geneva *rue des Plantaporrets #290-619*

Grindelwald *Terrasenweg #531-009*

Interlaken *Aareweg am See #224-353*

Kreuzlingen *Promenadenstr. 7 #752-663*

Lausanne *chemin du Muguet 1 #265-782*

Lucerne *Sedelstr. 12 #368-800*

Montreux *passage de l'Auberge 8 #634-934*

Pontresina *Tolais #67223*

St. Gallen *25 Speicherstr. #243-444*

St. Moritz (Bad) *Via Surpunt 60 #33969*

Winterthur *Hegifeldstr. 125 #273-840*

Yverdon *rue du Parc 14 #211-233*

Zermatt *#672-320*

Zug *General Guisan Str. #215-354*

Zurich *Mutschellenstr. 114 #482-3544*

RAILROAD TIMETABLES

Zurich to:

Amsterdam	7.57—17.46
Frankfurt	9.57—14.17
Paris	9.57—16.16
Rome	8.39—19.13
Venice	8.39—16.38
Vienna	9.26—19.00

Austria

The period between the 10th and 18th centuries was marked with periodic pogroms and expulsions for Jews of Austria. Following the 1782 Edict of Tolerance by Emperor Joseph II, Jews were no longer required to pay special Jewish taxes and were no longer required to wear distinctive dress. Complete emancipation was achieved in 1867. However, anti- Semitism, as an official political policy, was blossoming as well. This was culminated during the second World War. After the war, Vienna became a staging-point for some 200,000 Jews who were headed for Israel. During the 1970s, Vienna, again, became the staging point for a mass influx of Jews. This time, it was the "entrance-point" into the free world for several thousand Russian Jews. There are today about 12,000 Jews living in Austria.

SYNAGOGUES

Graz *Grieskai 58 #86327*

Innsbruck *Zollerstr. 1 #6892*

Linz *Bethlehemstr. 26 #22835*

Salzburg *Mertensstr. 7 #72228*

Vienna *Grunangergasse 1 #52-83-31*
Templegasse 3 #24-92-62
Fleischmarkt 1
Judenplatz 8 #66-41-53
Riemergasse 9
Schiffgasse 8 #35-28-112

Vienna Jewish Museum *Bauerfeldgasse 4*

MIKVEHS

Salzburg *Lasserstr. 8*

Vienna *Templegasse 3 #24-92-62*
Fleischmarkt 22 #52-52-62
Lilienbrunngasse 19 #26-88-44

KOSHER PROVISIONS

Vienna *(grocer) Reisnerstr. 50 #73-37-15*
(restaurant) Hollandstr. 3 #33-35-65
(restaurant) Liechtensteinstr. 12 #34-41-86
(butcher) Grosse Pfarrgasse 6 #35-35-46

AMERICAN EXPRESS OFFICES

Innsbruck *Brixnerstr. 3 #22491*

Klagenfurt *Leutschacherstr. 17 #33520*

Linz *Buergerstr. 14 #66-90-13*

Salzburg *5 Mozartplatz #42501*

Vienna *Kaerntnerstr. 21 #520544*

YOUTH HOSTELS

Innsbruck *Reichenauerstr. 147 #46179*
Rennweg 17b #25814
Sillg. 8a #31311

Linz *Stanglhofweg 3 #664434*
Bluterstr. 23 #237078

Salzburg *Aignerstr. 34 #23248*
Josef Preis Allee 18 #42670
Glockengasse 8 #76241

Vienna *Friedrich Engelsplatz 24 #338294*
Myrthengasse 7 #937167
Lechnerstr. 12 #731494

RAILROAD TIMETABLES

Vienna to:

Amsterdam	7.20—20.54
Berlin	9.30—22.12
Copenhagen	7.20—6.45
London	20.50—18.58
Paris	8.00—23.15
Rome	7.55—23.50
Stockholm	7.20—9.00 (next day)
Venice	7.55—16.54
Zurich	7.00—16.28

Prague, Czechoslovakia

ENTERING EASTERN (COMMUNIST) EUROPE

You must have a valid passport. You must have a visa, which can be acquired in the consulates of each respective country. These consulates are located in the capitals of all western European countries. The addresses of these consulates can be ascertained from local travel agencies. The visa costs about $20 and can be acquired within an hour. Be sure to have your passport and two identification photos before going to the consulates. There are instant portrait machines in all European cities.

You must purchase your train ticket before boarding the inter- city train to Prague. The Eurailpass is not valid in East Europe. You can, however, use it up to the border. As the train crosses the border into Communist Europe, you will notice the heavy barbed-wire fortifications. There are mine fields on the Communist side of the border. There are watchtowers and spotlights. The train will now stop for about two hours. Armed soldiers will be stationed outside the train, at each door. A soldier will walk a German shepherd dog alongside the entire train, which will check and sniff under each car. At twenty- minute intervals, border-control inspectors will enter your train compartment and ask for passports and visas. You are required to change about $25 into their local currency on board the train. There is a special inspector for that operation. It is forbidden to either bring-in or take-out local (Communist) currency. You can change your foreign currency at your hotel in Prague or at an official state-run bank. Do not change money on the streets!

There will be many people approaching you and asking to "change money." These people might be Communist agents!

After the inspectors pass, there are two agents dressed in jump-suit overalls, who look like auto mechanics. These men will come with flashlights and check under your seats and will actually dismantle part of the roof-panels (near the rest rooms) and look to see if anyone is hiding-out in these crawl spaces.

The train journey from Nuremberg to Prague takes about nine hours. It is worth every minute. The scenery along the way is breathtaking. You will pass little villages that resemble the *shtetlech* of hundreds of years ago. There are spectacular wild-flowers and hundreds of acres of beer hops, which will ultimately become the world-renowned "Pilsner" beer.

It is highly recommended to book hotel reservations in advance. This can be done in Western Europe. The major (English-speaking) hotels in Prague are the Inter-Continental and the Olympic Hotels. The Inter-Continental Hotel is a three-minute walk from the historic Jewish Museum and Jewish Cemetery. Please note that before your return train trip, it is highly recommended to reserve a seat on that train (even if you already have a return ticket). Trains are usually very crowded in the summer. Just show your return ticket to the ticket clerk in the train station the day before your departure, and she will assign a seat number on the ticket. There is no charge for this service.

Very few people in Prague speak English. German, however, is understood by many of the older people. There is a Jewish tour guide who will be most happy to welcome you into Prague. His name is Mr.Roth and can be contacted through the Cedok Government Tourist Office.

Prague

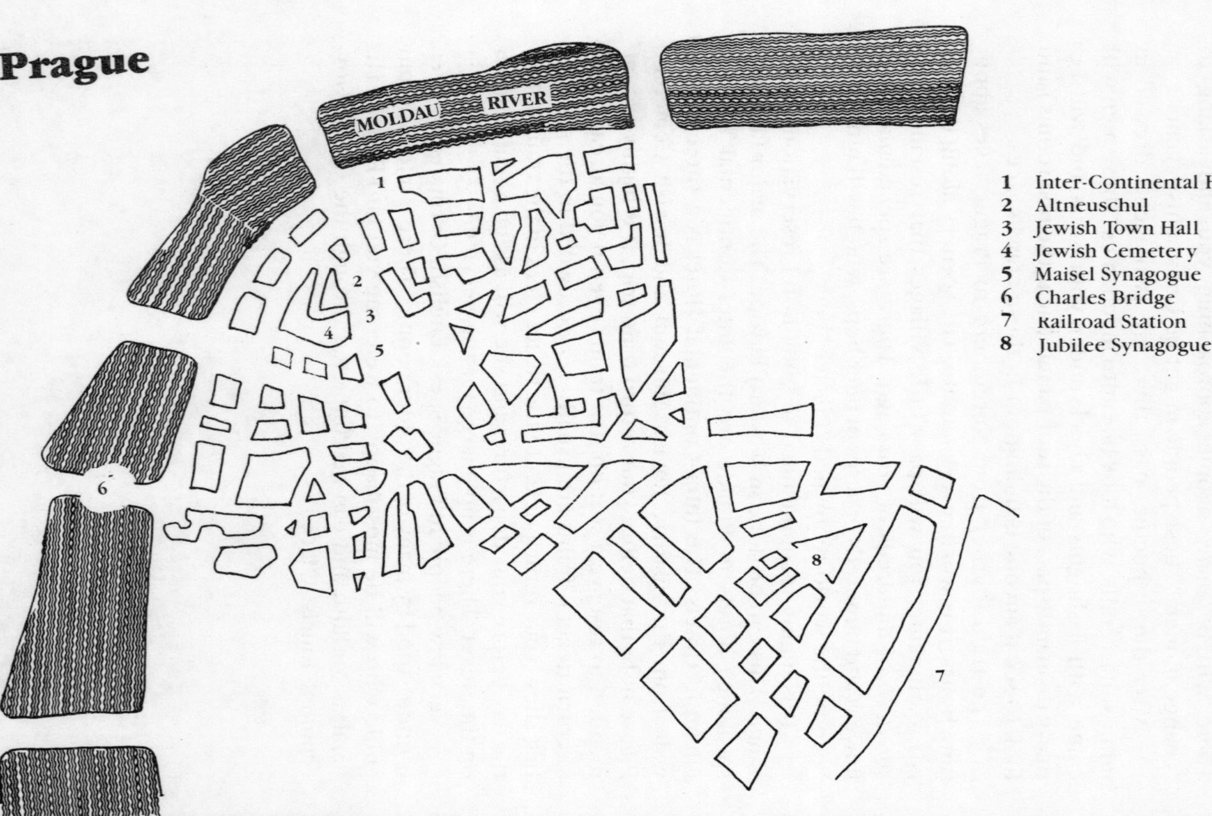

MOLDAU
RIVER
1
2
3
4
5
6
7
8
1 Inter-Continental Hotel
2 Altneuschul
3 Jewish Town Hall
4 Jewish Cemetery
5 Maisel Synagogue
6 Charles Bridge
7 Railroad Station
8 Jubilee Synagogue

PRAGUE

Jewish settlement in Czechoslovakia (Bohemia) dates from 906. Jewish merchants traveling from the Rhineland on their way to the Near East founded a community on the left bank of the Vltava (Moldau) River at Prague.

Prague's medieval Jewish community did not live in a ghetto, that is, a closed area of enforced residence. Jews paid heavy taxes to the kings. In return, the royal charters granted the Jewish community autonomy in its social, political, legal, and religious affairs. It was a self-governing entity whose basic institutions were the synagogue, the council (*kahal*), the courts, the schools, and charitable societies. The Jewish town had its own judges, town hall, mayor, flag, police and fire departments.

The Jews of the Czech lands lived with severe disadvantages and often with threat of violence. When the First Crusaders swept southward from the Rhine in 1096, they inflicted heavy casualties on the Jews of Prague. In 1389, members of the Prague clergy spread stories of Jewish blasphemy and desecration of the Host. They encouraged angry mobs to ransack, loot, and burn the Jewish quarter. Hundreds of Jews were murdered; numerous women and children were forcibly baptised. A special prayer written by Rabbi Avigdor Karo, commemorating this massacre, is still recited by the Jews of Prague on Yom Kippur.

The Golden Age of Prague Jewry lasted for nearly two hundred years. From the beginning of the 16th century, Prague was a famous center of Jewish scholarship and rabbinical learning under the inspiration of Rabbi Judah Loew ben Bezalel (the Maharal mai Prague) and Rabbi Yom Tov Lipmann Heller. Other prominent personalities of Prague include Marcus Mordecai Meisel, banker and adviser to the Hapsburg emperor and David Gans, the chronicler, astronomer, and mathematician.

During World War II, the Nazis created the world's greatest collection of Judaica. Hitler wished to create a Jewish museum which would be in memory of the extinct Jewish people. He ordered the confiscation of Jewish libraries, archives, religious artifacts, and all manner of personal property throughout all Nazi-occupied territories. They were to be shipped to the old Jewish quarter of Prague and stored in the ancient synagogues, former Jewish homes and warehouses. Thousands of Torahs, silver ornaments, Torah mantles and ark covers, as well as gold wedding bands, violins, and pianos, were shipped to Prague after the Jewish communities of Bohemia, Moravia, and Slovakia were annihilated. Today, the Prague State Jewish Museum contains that "precious legacy" bequeathed by European Jewry.

There are about 13,000 Jews living in Czechoslovakia, of which 3,000 live in the city of Prague.

ALTNEUSCHUL 2 Cervana St.

Built ca. 1265, the Altneuschul (Old-New Synagogue) is the oldest extant synagogue in Europe. It is still used by the Jewish community of Prague. It is designed in the Gothic style. The main hall is divided into two naves of three bays each by rectangular piers which rise to support the rib-vaulted ceiling. An impression of soaring verticality is achieved despite the smallness of space (15m x 9m) through the lowering of the floor level below that of the adjacent street. This device, often used by architects to circumvent ecclesiastical restrictions placed on the height of synagogues during the Middle Ages, was intended to diminish Jewish houses of worship in comparison with churches.

Over the centuries, various additions were made to the original building, including a vestibule and a women's synagogue with apertures opening on the main hall. In the 15th century, the building's distinctive crenellated gable was added, and the original stone bimah, was replaced by a wooden one with a wrought-iron superstructure that fills the central space between the two main piers. On the bimah hangs a scarlet flag embroidered with a Star of David and a Swedish hat. This banner was presented to the Jews of Prague by Ferdinand III in 1648, in appreciation of their role in the defense of the city against the Swedes. The banner was customarily carried by the Jews at the head of processions on festive occasions. The chair on the bimah always remains empty. This chair is said to have been used by Rabbi Loew in the 16th century, when he preached here. The attic of the Altneuschul is supposed to house the remains of Rabbi Loew's *golem*.

Rabbi Loew (the Maharal) served the community for thirty-six years. He founded a yeshiva which gained international prominence. He encouraged the pursuit of scientific study, as long as this did not contradict the "principles of Judaism." Sometime after his death, the career of the Maharal entered the worlds of

The Altneuschul in Prague is the oldest synagogue in Europe.

both Jewish and Czech folklore. In both the Jewish and non-Jewish literary sources, the Maharal is credited with having created an artificial being out of clay, a *golem*, by virtue of a magical act, involving the use of the Holy name. The tale of a monster who was summoned to life by a wise and righteous rabbi and defended the Jewish community against attacks from the outside, gave eloquent expression to the hopes and fears of East European Jewry, following the Chmielnicki massacres of 1648.

The name Altneuschul, Old-New Synagogue, refers, according to many authorities, to the renovation of an old synagogue, Altschul. There is a tale, however, which describes the name *altenai* schul, meaning the "on condition that" synagogue. It seems that originally this synagogue was built with stones from the Holy Temple of Jerusalem. But when the Messiah comes, this building will be torn down and the original stones will be brought back to Jerusalem for the rebuilding of the Holy Temple.

There are more than 10,000 tombstones in the old Jewish cemetery of Prague.

Some famous personalities associated with Czech history include Gustav Mahler, Sigmund Freud, Franz Kafka, Issac Mayer Wise, and Louis D.Brandeis.

OLD JEWISH CEMETERY

The old Jewish cemetery is a cramped, urban enclosure of veritable hills, overgrown in the spring and summer and crowded with tombstones. The community buried its dead here from the 14th to the end of the 18th century, but long before then, had exhausted all the available space. The solution was to cover existing graves with earth, bury the new dead on a second level, and top the surface with tombstones from the two layers combined. No one knows exactly how many times this process was repeated before the cemetery was closed in 1787; perhaps as many as twelve! Hence, one has the feeling of walking up and down hills when visiting the cemetery. The visual image is of tombstones packed together, leaning on one another, indicating the names and dates of the deceased but hiding their precise location. There are more than 10,000 tombstones in the cemetery. Here are buried: the Maharal (Rabbi Loew), Marcus Mordecai Maisel, Rabbi Avigdor Karo, and David Gans.

CEREMONIAL HALL 3 Jachymova St.

This Romanesque structure, originally erected as a mortuary, separates the Klaus Synagogue from the old Jewish cemetery. It became a Jewish museum in 1926. In this museum are the caftan and banner of Solomon Molcho, the false Messiah of the 16th century, who bequeathed his flag and robe to the Prague Jewish community before he was condemned to death as an heretic during the inquisition in 1532.

KLAUS SYNAGOGUE Josefovska St.

The largest of the existing synagogues in Prague, was founded in the end of the 16th century by Rabbi Judah Loew ben Bezalel, the Maharal. The synagogue contained a mikveh and rabbincal school. It was rebuilt in 1694 and then included a two-storied women's section opening onto the main hall. It was in this building that the Nazis started assembling tens of thousands of Jewish ritual objects for their museum of the extinct Jewish people.

PINKAS SYNAGOGUE Josefovska St.

Adjoining the old Jewish cemetery, the Pinkas Synagogue was built in 1535 on the site of a 10th century synagogue. On the walls of the Pinkas Synagogue are inscribed the names of 77,297 Bohemian and Moravian Jews who were killed by the Nazis during World War II. This building is now part of the State Jewish Museum.

SPANISH SYNAGOGUE Dusni St.

Built in 1867 on the site of Prague's oldest synagogue, the Altschul, the Spanish Synagogue is decorated in the Moorish style. As part of the State Jewish Museum, there are eight thousand synagogue textiles, formerly used in now-destroyed synagogues.

MAISEL SYNAGOGUE Maislova St.

Built in the 16th century, the Maisel Synagogue was commissioned by the mayor of the Jewish community, Marcus Mordecai Maisel. The ark, bimah, and synagogue furnishings were removed by the Nazis during the war. In its place, today, is an exhibition of Judaic ritual objects, including spice boxes, menorahs, Torah crowns, and pointers.

JEWISH TOWN HALL 18 Maislova St.

The Baroque Jewish Town Hall was built by the mayor of the Jewish community, Marcus Mordecai Maisel, at the end of the 16th century. It was rebuilt in 1754, after a fire. At that time, a unique clock with Hebrew letters for numerals, was added. The clock runs backwards (as Hebrew is read). The building contains the so-called High Synagogue, also built by Maisel, but no longer in use. The headquarters of the Council of Jewish Religious Communities is also housed in the Town Hall. There is a kosher restaurant at the street-level entrance which is open from 11.30 a.m to 1.00 p.m daily, including Sabbath and Jewish Festivals. It is closed on Sundays. For further information call 231-8664 or 231-0909.

CHARLES BRIDGE

In 1609, a Jew was accused of desecrating the crucifix and, as punishment, the Jewish community was forced to pay for affixing the Hebrew words, *kadosh, kadosh, kadosh, etc.* onto the crucifix of a statue on the Charles Bridge, in letters of gold.

JUBILEE SYNAGOGUE 7 Jerusalem St.

The Moorish Revival synagogue, built in the 1890s, is still functioning. It is located two blocks from the main railroad station.

AMERICAN EXPRESS OFFICE

Prague Cedok *NA Prikope 18 #22-42-51-9*

YOUTH HOSTELS

Prague *Zitna 12*
Spartakiadni 5

Budapest, Hungary

GREAT SYNAGOGUE Dohany utca 2

The largest synagogue in Europe was designed by Ludwig von Foerster. The cornerstone was laid in September, 1854. The synagogue measures 56.1m in length, 26.5m in width, and 26m high internally, with the Moorish twin onion-domed minarets 43.6m in height on the front. It took five years to complete. It is still the synagogue with the largest seating capacity in Europe, having 1,492 seats for men in rows across the nave and the two aisles and 1,472 seats for women in the two tiers of galleries which run along the north, south, and west sides. Iron piers support the three great semicircular lobate arches over the north and south galleries; twin pulpits rest against the piers on either side of the first and second bays. Liszt and Saint-Saëns both played on the organ of this synagogue. The design of the Plum Street Temple of Cincinnati, Ohio (1866), the first Moorish synagogue in the United States, and the Central Synagogue of New York City (1872), were both influenced in their designs by the Great Synagogue of Budapest. There are services only on the Sabbath and on Jewish Festivals. On Yom Kippur, there are 6,000 people attending services—standing-room only! The street in back of the Great Synagogue houses a Jewish Rest Home and a kosher restaurant.

JEWISH MUSEUM Dohany utca

Adjoining the Great Synagogue is the Jewish Museum which stands on the site of the house where Dr.Theodor Herzl, father of

Exterior and interior views of the largest synagogue in Europe, the Dohany utca Synagogue in Budapest, Hungary.

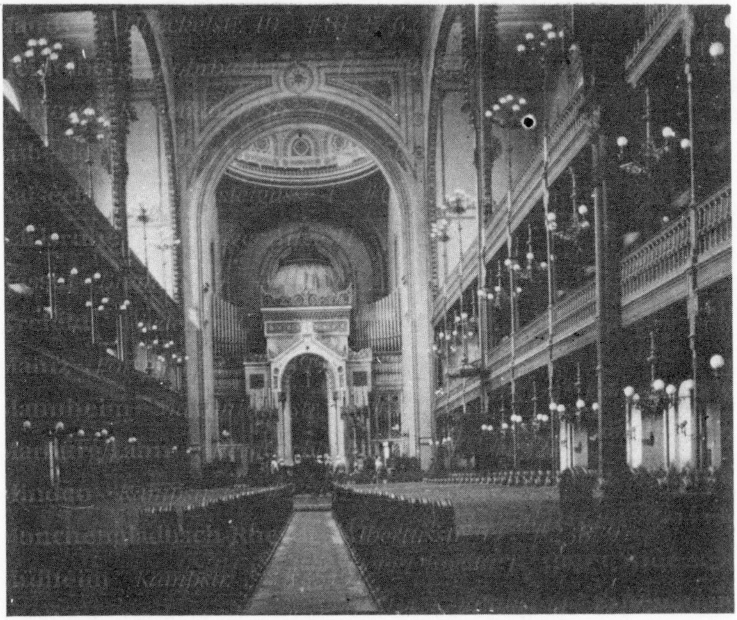

political Zionism, was born. The museum was opened in 1909 and contains displays, photos, drawings, documents, artifacts, and religious objects dealing with the history of Hungarian Jewry. During World War II, the synagogue was surrounded by a wooden fence. This marked the edge of the Budapest ghetto. The synagogue itself became a concentration camp. Behind the museum is a courtyard/cemetery where 2,000 Jews were shot. They were buried in a mass grave in the courtyard.

JEWISH THEOLOGICAL SEMINARY Jezsef Korut 27

The only rabbinical seminary in all of Eastern Europe, including Russia, was organized in the 1890s. All rabbis for all of the Communist countries are trained in this academy. Last year, there were only twenty-five graduates. The seminary building houses a Jewish library containing more than 60,000 volumes. Dr. Sandor Scheiber is the dean of the seminary and also is the director of the Jewish museum.

There are 80,000 Jews living in Hungary, with 65,000 living in Budapest.

SYNAGOGUE

Budapest Central Orthodox Synagogue *Kazinczy utca 29*

MIKVEH

Budapest *Kazinczy utca 16 #221-172*

KOSHER RESTAURANTS

Budapest *Dob utca 35 #421-072*
Katona Jozsef utca 9 #121-372

AMERICAN EXPRESS OFFICE

Budapest Ibusz Travel Bureau *Petofi Ter 3 #184-848*

YOUTH HOSTELS

Budapest *Irinyi u 7 #250-227*
Beethoven u 7 #158-891
Becsi u 104 #682-036

Belgium

Jews lived in Belgium since the 13th century. Marrano Jews from Spain and Portugal found refuge in Belgium after the Inquisition. After 1714, Belgium became part of Holland and, in 1794, became part of France. Belgium became independent in 1831. In that year, there were 3,000 Jews in the country. The diamond industry became a dominant industry in Antwerp after 1880, when thousands of Jewish refugees fled from the pogroms of Eastern Europe. Antwerp is the site of the Diamond Bourse (Exchange). Walking along the Pelikanstraat, one of Antwerp's major thoroughfares, you will see many chassidim, who are diamond dealers, cutters, polishers, and setters. This Diamond Bourse has international connections with diamond centers in New York City, Israel, and Johannesburg. A visitor to the Bourse must "know somebody" in the exchange in order to gain entrance. There are about 41,000 Jews living in Belgium today. In recent years, there have been several terrorist attacks against the Jewish community of Belgium. A dramatic outcome of these incidents is the new synagogue designed in the suburbs of Brussels. It resembles a 17th century wooden synagogue of Poland (but looks more like a pagoda). All of the windows in this new synagogue are filled with bullet-proof glass!

In the summer, most of Belgium's Jewish community goes to the seaside resort town of Knokke, Belgium's equivalent to New York's Catskills.

SYNAGOGUES

Antwerp ISRAELITISCHE GEMEENTE
Terliststr 35 #235-41-47
Bouwmeesterstr (1893 Moorish Revival building)
65 Isabellalei
Terlistr 35
Vanden Nestei
Hovenierstr 31

ISRAELITISCHE ORTHODOXE GEMEENTE
Oostenstr 43 #233-55-67
van Leriusstr 54
(Belz) van Spangenstr 6
(Ger) Antoon van Dykstr 43
(Lubavitch) Plantijn Moretuslei 49
van Leriusstr 37
(Satmar) Jacob Jabobstr 6
(Vishnitz) Brialmontlei 16
Consciencestr 40
Oostenstr 29
Marsstr 40
van Leriusstr 22
Mercatorstr 56

Brussels *20 avenue Mozart*
73 rue de Thy #648-38-37
rue de Chapeau #521-12-89
101 avenue Stalingrad
3 rue Houzeau de Lehaye
32 rue de la Regence
67a rue de la Clinique
126 rue Rogier
47 rue du Pavillon #215-21-38

LIBERAL
96 avenue Kersbeek #345-59-92

Charleroi *56 rue Pige au Croly*

Ghent *14 Savaenstr*

Knocke *38 avenue Jean Volders #537-06-08*

Liege *19 rue L.Frederic*

Mons *49 Grand Rue*

Ostend *10 Maastrichtplein*

MIKVEHS

Antwerp *Steenbokstr 22 #239-75-88*
van Diepenbeecksstr 42 #239-09-65

Brussels *67a rue de la Clinique #521-12-89*

KOSHER RESTAURANTS

Antwerp *Simonstr 10* #232-60-42 Dresdner
Pelikanstr 86 #239-09-65 (Diamond Bourse)
Lange Kievitstr 49 Moskowitz
Nerviersstr 12 #39-39-11
Lange Leemstr 186
Hovenierstr 53
Korte Kievitstr
Gelkop *Van Leriusstr. 28 #233-07-53 (mon-thu 6-8 p.m. & sun 12 3 p.m.)*
Vestingstr 68
(bakery) Mercatorstr 20 #232-62-78
(bakery) Pelikanstr 102
Kleinblatt *(bakery) Provincierstr. & Wippstr.*

Brussels *(butcher) 37 avenue Jean Volders #537-06-08*
(bakery) 62 rue de Suede #537-16-79
(Lubavitch) Rabbi Chaikin 1a avenue Reine Marie Henritte #87867

AMERICAN EXPRESS OFFICES

Antwerp *87 Meir #232-59-20*

Brussels *2 place Louise #512-17-40*
avenue des Louisirs #241-87-62

YOUTH HOSTELS

Antwerp *Eric Sasselaan 2 #238-02-73*

Brugge *4/Assebroeke, Baron Ruzettelaan 143 #352679*

Brussels *Heilig Geeststr 2 #511-04-36*

Ghent *Sint Pietersplein 12 #22-50-67*

Liege *rue du Parc 73 #41-35-19*

Ostend *Langestr 82 #70-54-84*

RAILROAD TIMETABLES

Brussels to:

Amsterdam	9.10–12.07
Berlin	9.48–20.40
Copenhagen	6.48–19.45
London	9.59–14.31
Paris	10.10–13.00
Rome	18.02–13.45
Vienna	7.48–21.28
Zurich	12.12–19.57

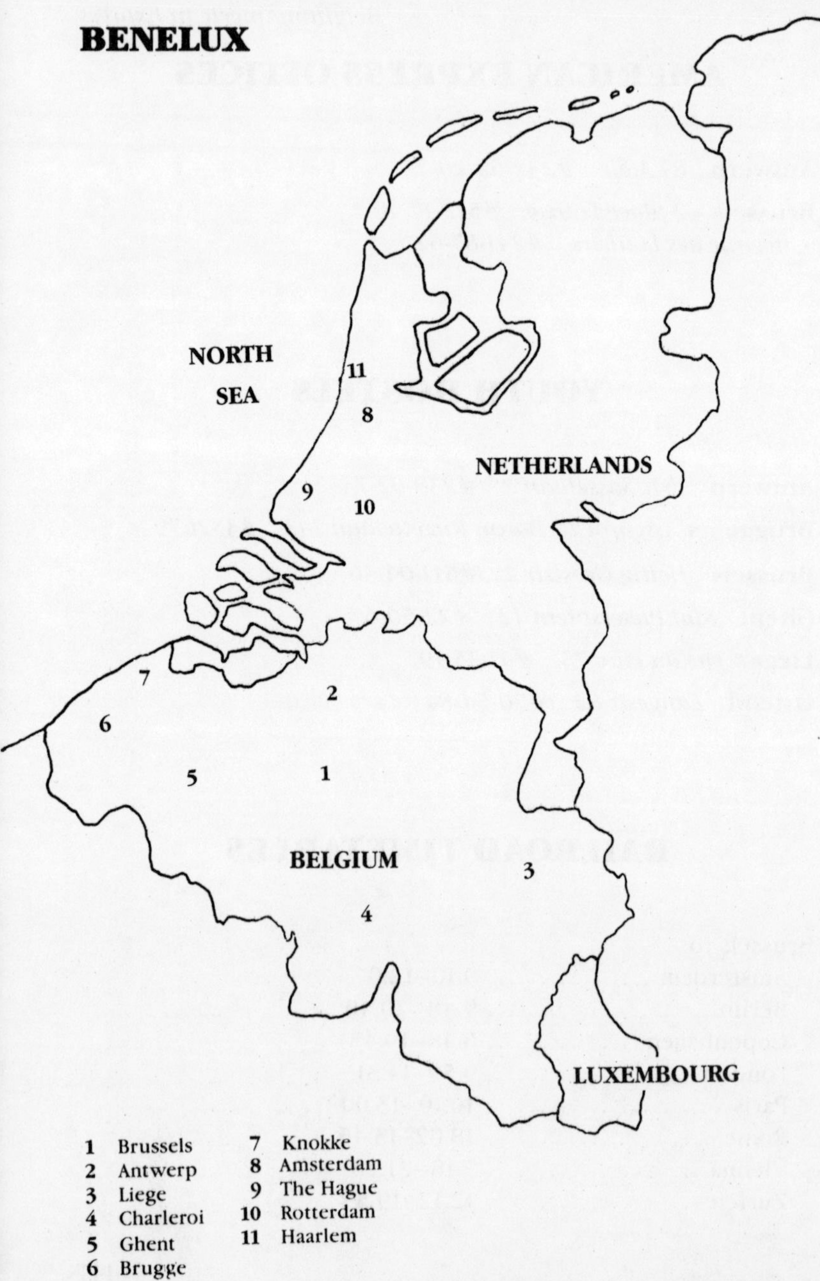
BENELUX
NORTH SEA
NETHERLANDS
BELGIUM
LUXEMBOURG
11
8
9
10
7
2
6
5
1
3
4
1 Brussels
2 Antwerp
3 Liege
4 Charleroi
5 Ghent
6 Brugge
7 Knokke
8 Amsterdam
9 The Hague
10 Rotterdam
11 Haarlem

Netherlands (Holland)

The first Jewish communities in Holland were organized in the end of the 16th century by Marranos, secret Jews, fleeing the persecutions of the Inquisitions of Spain and Portugal. Holland was then a Protestant country and offered the Jews religious freedom. The Jews encouraged trade and commerce. They introduced the diamond, tobacco and silk industries, opened sugar refineries, and played a key role in developing Holland's overseas commerce. They had mercantile and familial connections in Venice, Italy, Cochin, India, and helped organize the Dutch East Indies and Dutch West Indies Companies. The Dutch West Indies Company had branches in Recife, Brazil, Willemstad, Curacao, and New Amsterdam, New Holland. New Amsterdam later became the city of New York.

The 17th century was Holland's Golden Age. There were great accomplishments in literature, philosophy, and the arts. There were noted rabbis, scholars, poets and scientists. Amsterdam was then known as the "New Jerusalem." The original Jewish settlers were Sephardic, but after 1630, there was a large influx of Ashkenazic Jews from Germany, Poland, and Lithuania. The great synagogues, Sephardic and Ashkenazic, were built during this Golden Age of Holland.

In 1795, Napoleon ruled Holland, granted complete civil equality, which enabled the first country in Europe to elect Jews to its parliament. During World War II, some Christian citizens risked their lives to hide Jews from the Nazis.

There are today about 30,000 Jews living in Holland; 20,000 of them live in Amsterdam. There is a Holocaust memorial in Amsterdam, at Plantage Middenlaan 24, which was once a Yiddish theatre and was the assembling point of all Jews who were to be deported to the concentration camps.

AMSTERDAM

GREAT PORTUGUESE SYNAGOGUE
Mr. Visserplein 3

The Sephardic community commissioned the master-builder, Elias Bouman, to design their *esnoga* (pronounced esnochah) or synagogue in 1671. The magnificent structure, completed in 1675, the congregation's second major synagogue, was designed in the Classical idiom, best described as "Protestant Baroque." The esnoga was built, as were all of the buildings in Amsterdam, on pilings and above the canals. There is no cellar in the building. Four main Ionic columns, symbolic of the four Matriarchs of the Jewish faith, support the great wooden barrel vault. There are twelve smaller columns, symbolic of the twelve tribes of Israel, which support the women's galleries. The ark (*heychal*) and bimah (*taybah*) are made of jacaranda wood imported from Brazil. During the day, natural light floods the synagogue through many windows. During the evening, since electricity has never been installed, the only source of light is candle-power. The esnoga is a breathtaking sight, with its magnificent brass candelabra as well as its 613 brass candle-tapers aglow. The number 613 is symbolic of the number of commandments of the Torah. The main sanctuary is only used for evening services on Jewish Festivals and on

AMSTERDAM

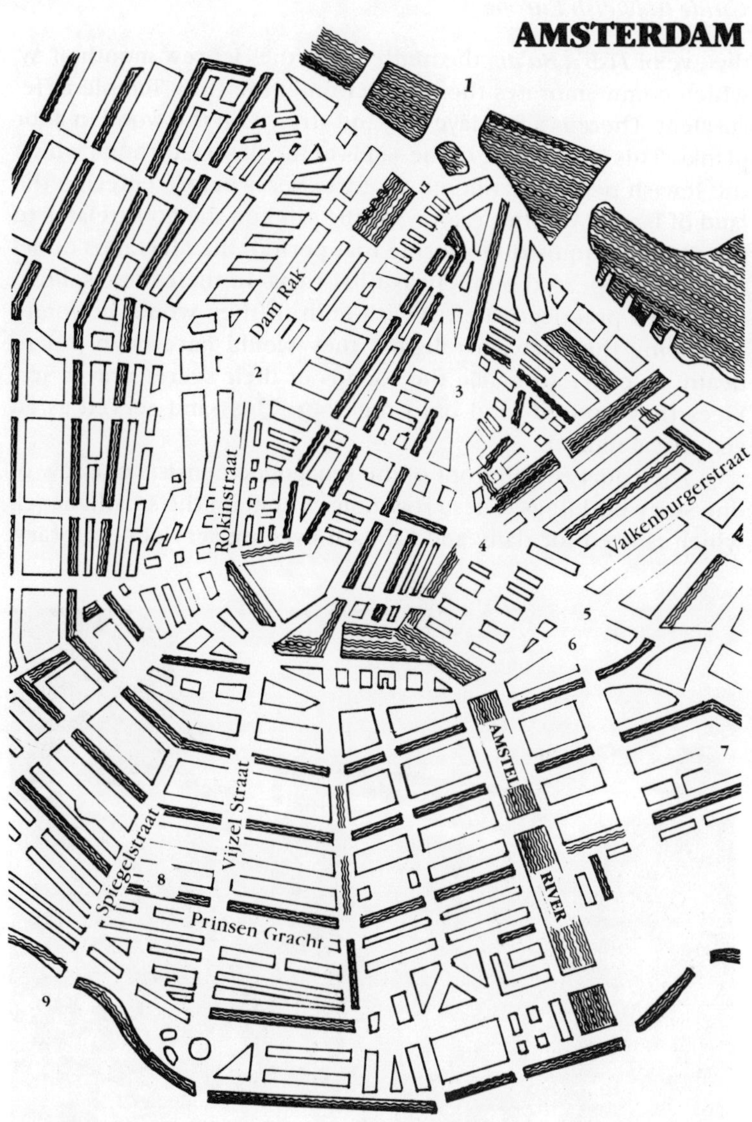

1 Railroad Station
2 Dam
3 Jewish Museum—Nieuwmarkt
4 Rembrandt House
5 Great Portuguese Synagogue
6 High German Synagogue
7 Synagogue (148 Nieuwe Kerkstr.)
8 Anne Frank House
9 Rijksmuseum

the eve of *Tish'a Ba'av*, the ninth day of the Hebrew month of Av, which commemorates the destruction of the Holy Temple in Jerusalem. There is a fine layer of sand strewn on the wooden floor planks. This is symbolic of the sands of the desert, through which the Jewish people wandered for forty years before entering the land of Israel. Another reason for the sand on the floor relates to the Spanish Inquisition. During that period, the Marranos or secret Jews appeared publicly as Christians. In their homes, however, they practiced their Jewish faith. If they would be found practicing their Jewish religion, they would have been put to death. In order to muffle the sounds of their secret prayer services they poured sand onto the floor. This sand served as an acoustical muffler.

The courtyard in front of the synagogue consists of a row of one-story buildings. These row-houses contain the small chapel, which is used for daily and Sabbath evening services, a library,

The Great Portuguese Synagogue of Amsterdam.

classrooms, the rabbi's and sextant's living quarters, and a mikveh.

When there was a funeral in the 17th century, the body was cleansed in the mikveh, then taken downstairs, to the canal (since there is no cellar), put on a barge and rowed to the ancient Jewish cemetery in Ouderkerk.

Once a year, the rabbi, sexton and rabbi of the congregation went below the esnoga with an engineer on a barge to inspect the structural systems of the building. There is a 300 year old *succah* in the courtyard of the synagogue. It was originally designed to be prefabricated, but due to its age, it has now been set up permanently on this site.

Be prepared to go through a security check at the front gate of the synagogue. There have been attempts to bomb the Great Portuguese Synagogue. All handbags and cameras are stored in lockers at the front gate. Photography is strictly forbidden. Services at the Great Portuguese Synagogue follow the Western Sephardic ritual. Men are seated downstairs and women are seated upstairs. Services are very formal. The officials of the congregation wear top hats. The sextant wears a long black coat and a bicorne, a cocked hat in the style of the Napoleonic era. The chazan or cantor, also wears a long black coat, but wears a white cloth over his chest and a three cornered round hat, similar to the attire of 17th century Calvanist clergymen. The chazan always wears his *tallit* or prayer shawl over his head. The service at the Great Portuguese Synagogue has not changed in over three hundred years. The tradition continues . . .

During World War II, before the Nazis entered the city of Amsterdam, the Dutch authorities declared the Great Portuguese Synagogue a national monument. The Nazis had a policy of not touching a national monument or museum. The entire building was therefore spared from destruction. The small chapel with panelled walls is like a room in a 17th century private house, except for the screened women's gallery behind and above the west wall. The ark is a Dutch Baroque armoire of the period, the work of a master cabinetmaker.

The Spanish and Portuguese synagogues of Bevis Marks, London. Willemstad, Curacao, New Amsterdam (New York City), Newport, Rhode Island (Touro Synagogue), Philadelphia, and Gibraltar are all modelled after the mother esnoga of Amsterdam. Although the exteriors of these buildings vary greatly, since they reflect the local architectural styles, the interiors are all designed with the Amsterdam esnoga as the prototype.

GREAT ASHKENAZIC SYNAGOGUE
Jonas Daniel Meyerplein

Built in 1730 by the German and Polish Jews, the "High German" or "Hoog Duitsch" Synagogue was not declared a national monument by the Dutch government before World War II. The interior was desecrated and was used as a stable. There are now plans to restore the building and use it as a Jewish Museum.

JEWISH HISTORICAL MUSEUM Nieuwmarkt

Located in the old Weighing House, the Jewish Historical Museum has a fine collection of ritual and religious objects, paintings by Jewish artists, and valuable manuscripts. There are now plans to move this Jewish Museum into the old Great Ashkenazic Synagogue, on Jonas Daniel Meyerplein, which is presently being restored. There are former synagogue buildings located at 109 Rapenburgerstr. (opposite the flea market), and at Plantage Kerkl (opposite the Amsterdam zoo).

ANNE FRANK HOUSE 263 Prinsengracht

Many Dutch Christians hid Jews in secret rooms in old warehouses in Amsterdam during World War II. From July, 1942, to August, 1944, Anne Frank, a Jewish teenager, and her family went into hiding from the Nazis. It was in this secret attic, in the annex of a warehouse, where Anne Frank wrote her moving diary. It was on August 1, 1944 that Anne wrote her last entry in her diary. On August 4,1944, a truck with German police and their Dutch cohorts, appeared at the door. They walked straight to the bookcase which concealed the entrance to the secret attic, shouted "Open up!" and seized the terrified hideaways. A German policeman ordered everyone to hand over their jewelry and valuables. He took Mr. Frank's attache case, which contained Anne's notebooks, shook the contents out onto the floor and put in what he wanted to take with him. Anne's diary was left behind. The hideaways were carried off, first to Westerbork and then to Auschwitz. All of the people who were hid in the attic perished in the camps except for Mr.Otto Frank, Anne's father. He returned after the war and found Anne's diary still lying on the floor. The Anne Frank House became a museum in 1957. It is open daily from 9.00 a.m to 5.00 p.m. For further information call 26-45-33.

RIJKSMUSEUM (NATIONAL GALLERY) Stadhouderskade

This is one of the world's great art galleries, containing nineteen of Rembrandt's paintings, including two of his most celebrated Jewish works—the portrait of Dr. Ephraim Bueno and "The Jewish Bride." Rembrandt lived and worked for seventeen years in the Jewish section of the city. Rembrandt's House is now a national shrine and is located at 4 Jodenbreestraat. There are several paintings in the Rijksmuseum by the Jewish Dutch painter, Josef Israels.

The Rijksmuseum is open daily, including Saturday. A ticket to the museum can be purchased before the Sabbath, and left at the door, thereby permitting Orthodox Jews access to the museum, without violating the Sabbath.

PORTUGUESE JEWISH CEMETERY

Located five miles south of Amsterdam, in the village of Ouderkerk, along the Amstel River, is the oldest landmark of Dutch Jewry, the *bet chaim* or Jewish cemetery. The oldest tombstone is dated 1616. The unique and elaborately carved tombstones are fine examples of sepulchral art, reflecting a wide variety of biblical scenes and Baroque ornamentation. Some graves are simple, but many marble stones and monuments have exceptionally beautiful and artistic reliefs with poetic inscriptions describing the ability and excellence of the interred.

There are many important personalities buried in this cemetery such as: Rabbi Manasseh ben Israel, the distinguished scholar who pleaded with Oliver Cromwell for the readmission of the Jews to England; Dr.Ephraim Bueno, the physician whose portrait was painted and etched by Rembrandt and Jan Lievens; Don Samuel Palache, the envoy of the king of Morocco, whose funeral procession in the Hague was accompanied by the royal dignitaries such as Prince Maurice of Holland; and Abigail da Penha, the model of Rembrandt's famous painting, "The Jewish Bride." Baruch Spinoza is not buried in this cemetery, although his parent's graves are here. The Jewish community excommunicated Baruch Spinoza for his unorthodox philosophical views, which were believed to threaten the entire Jewish community.

(Take the subway to Bijlmer station, then bus # 175 to Ouderkerk)

WESTERBORK

The site of the World War II concentration camp is located outside of Amsterdam. It was where over 110,000 Dutch Jews passed, on their way to the death camps in Germany and Poland.

ASHKENAZ SYNAGOGUE Jacob Obrechtplein

Designed in 1928 by Harry Elte, the Ashkenaz Synagogue incorporates the International style of architecture. This design was influenced by the works of Frank Lloyd Wright. The gallery over the entrance to the main sanctuary rests on square posts which stand on a continuous pedestal. These short pillars are decorated with abstract, geometric patterns in the style of Piet Mondrian, the Dutch painter who influenced modern design not only abroad, but also in his own country. Elte's treatment of the parabolic arch, which spans the niche of the ark, is quite exciting. He divided the broad soffit of the arch into three glazed channels. Lit from behind, these sweeping curves of stained glass focus the worshipper's attention on the ark, which occupies only a small area within the huge tympanum of the parabola. The tall "steeple" houses the water tower for the synagogue's mikveh.

SYNAGOGUES

Almelo *Molenkampspark 20 #2334*

Amersfoort *Drielingensteeg 2*

Amsterdam *(Sephardic) Mr.Visserplein 3 #24-53-51*
Jacob Obrechtplein
Lekstr 61
Gerard Dourstr 238
Linnaeusstr 105

G.v.d. Veenstr 26 (Kollel)
Nieuwe Kerkstr 149
Boechorst 26
Buitenveldert van der Boecjorstr 26

Straat van Messina
(Liberal) Soetendorpstr 8 #42-35-62
Groenhof 79 #41-25-80

Arnhem *Pastoorstr 17a #42-51-54*

Bussum *Kromme Englaan 1a*

Deventer *Lange Bisschopstr 19 #12594*

Dordrecht *Vrieseplein 17 #31817*

Eindhoven *Casimirstr 23 #51-12-53*

Enschede *Prinsestr 16 #23479*
(Liberal) #14123

Groningen *Folkingedstr 2 #123151*

Haarlem *Kenaupark 7 #326899*

Hilversum *30 Laanstr #13633*

Leeuwarden *Sacramenstr 19 #25123*

Leiden *Levendaal 16 #12-57-93*

Maastricht *Capucijnengang 2 #32320*

Middelburg *Nijverheidsweg 24 #13233*

Nijmegen *Gerard Nootstr 25 #23-19-38*

Rotterdam *Davidsplein 4 #66-97-65*

The Hague *Bezuidenhoutseweg 361 #83705*
(Liberal) Prinsessgracht 23 #55-94-86

Utrecht *Springweg 164*

Zwolle *Schoutenstr 14*

MIKVEHS

Amsterdam *Mr.Visserplein 3 #24-53-51*
Heinzestr 3 #71-84-18

Haarlem *Kenaupark 7 #32-68-99*

Rotterdam *Davidsplein 4 #66-97-65*

KOSHER PROVISIONS

Amsterdam Mensa de Lairessestr. 13
Sal Meyer *Scheldestr 45 #73-13-13*
Mouwes *Utrechtsestr 73 #23-50-53*
Theeboom *Tweede Sweelinckstr 5 #72-70-86*
Theeboom *Maastr 16 #72-48-27*
Marcus *Ferd.Bolstr 44 #71-98-81*
Mrs. Hertzberger *Plantage Westermanlaan 9c #23-46-84 (Sabbath meals)*

Rotterdam *(butcher) Bas Jungeriusstr 254 #85-17-08*

The Hague
Mouwes Gedempte Gracht 85 #(070) 63-11-08

AMERICAN EXPRESS OFFICES

Amsterdam *Damrak 6 #26-20-42*

Enschede *Boulevard 1945—107 #32-41-20*

Rotterdam *92 Meent #33-03-00*

The Hague *Venestr 20 #46-95-15*

YOUTH HOSTELS

Amsterdam *Kloveniersburgwal 97 #24-68-32*
Zandpad 5 #83-17-44

Haarlem *Jan Gijzenpad 3 #37-37-93*

Rotterdam *Rochussenstr 107 #36-57-63*

The Hague *Monstersweg 4 #25-06-00*

RAILROAD TIMETABLES

Amsterdam to:

Berlin	7.44–17.04
Copenhagen	8.03–19.29
London	8.58–16.31
Nice	7.00–22.49
Oslo	8.03–9.04 (next day)
Paris	7.00–13.00
Rome	8.58–7.58
Stockholm	8.03–8.47 (next day)
Vienna	6.59–21.25
Zurich	8.58–18.57

Luxembourg

There was Jewish settlement in Luxembourg as early as the 13th century. It was not until after the French Revolution that the first permanent Jewish community was established in 1808. During World War II, the Jewish community was wiped out. There are today about 1,200 Jews living in Luxembourg.

SYNAGOGUES

Esch-sur-Alzette *rue du Canal*

Luxembourg City *45 avenue Monterey #27261*

Mondorf les Bains Bristol Kosher Hotel *4 avenue Klein #681-15*

AMERICAN EXPRESS OFFICE

Luxembourg City Luxembourg Travel Office *41 avenue de la Liberte #2-489-966*

YOUTH HOSTEL

Luxembourg City *2 rue du Fort Olisy #26889*

Denmark

Denmark was the first of the Scandinavian countries to allow Jewish settlement. The earliest arrivals, in 1622, were a small group of Sephardic Jews from Amsterdam and Hamburg. They were granted full religious freedom and commercial privileges. Other Sephardic Jews followed, serving as financiers and jewelers to the royal family and the Danish nobility. The Talmudic scholar, Benjamin Musafia, was named King Christian IV's personal physician in 1646; and his son-in-law, Gabriel Milan, was appointed governor of the Danish West Indies (now the Virgin Islands) in 1684.

Danish hospitality to successive waves of Jewish immigrants has always been one of the country's proud traditions. The so-called "Viking Jews"—those who settled before 1903—were followed in that year by the Russian Jews fleeing the Kishinev pogroms. Then came other refugees from Eastern Europe after World War I and from Nazi Germany during the 1930s.

The Nazis had planned a round-up of Denmark's 8,000 Jews on October 1, 1943, the second day of Rosh Hashanah, when every Jew would be conveniently assembled in the synagogue or at home, easy prey for the special Kommando units of the Gestapo, which were hand-picked by Adolf Eichmann himself for their mission. German troopships were anchored in Copenhagen Harbor, ready to transport all the Jews to the death camps of central Europe.

But when the stormtroopers, in a series of carefully exe-

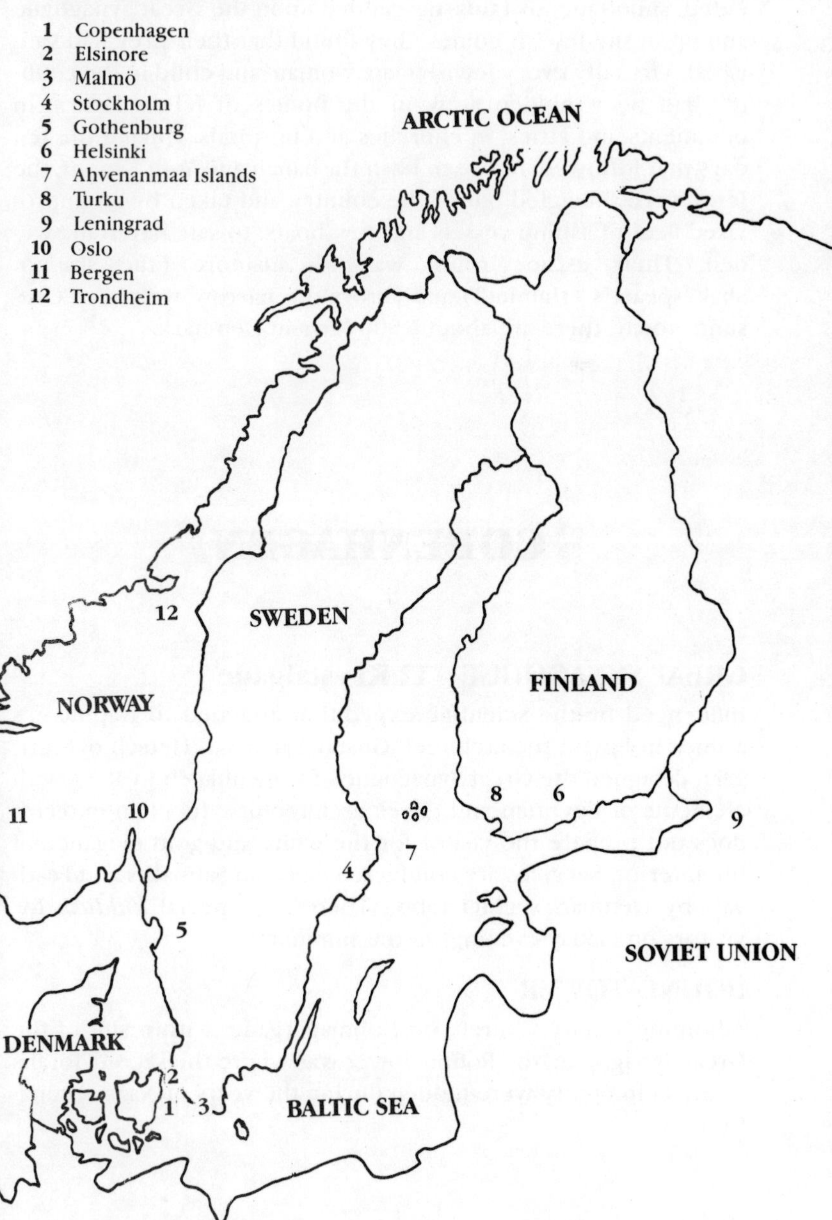
SCANDINAVIA
1 Copenhagen
2 Elsinore
3 Malmö
4 Stockholm
5 Gothenburg
6 Helsinki
7 Ahvenanmaa Islands
8 Turku
9 Leningrad
10 Oslo
11 Bergen
12 Trondheim
ARCTIC OCEAN
SWEDEN
FINLAND
NORWAY
SOVIET UNION
DENMARK
BALTIC SEA
12
11
10
8
6
9
7
4
5
2
1
3

cuted, simultaneous raids, descended upon the Great Synagogue and upon the Jewish homes, they found that their prey had vanished. Virtually every Jewish man, woman, and child in the country had been hidden away in the homes of fellow-Danes, in basements and attics, in churches and hospitals. During the ten days that followed, between Rosh Hashanah and Yom Kippur, the Jews were smuggled out of the country and taken by an improvised fleet of fishing vessels and row boats, to safe haven in Sweden. Their escape route was via Elsinore (the site of Shakespeare's "Hamlet") and across the narrow waters of Oresund. Today, there are about 7,500 Jews in Denmark.

COPENHAGEN

GREAT SYNAGOGUE 12 Krystalgade

Influenced by the scientific expedition attached to Napoleon's armies in Egypt, the architect, Gustav Friedrich Hetsch of Stuttgart, designed the Great Synagogue of Copenhagen in 1833 with elements of Egyptian and Greek architecture. Its plain exterior does not prepare the visitor for the white-and-gold elegance of the interior. Services are conducted daily, on Sabbaths and Festivals by Denmark's chief rabbi. There is a special *kiddush* for visitors on Friday evenings in the summer.

ROUND TOWER

Adjoining Trinity Church, on Kobmagergade, within site of the Great Synagogue, the Round Tower was where the sacred Torahs of the community were hidden during the years of Nazi occupation.

HOLMEN'S CHURCH BELFRY

The Holmen's Canal was the first station in the Danish Jews' underground escape-route to Sweden in 1943.

ROYAL DANISH LIBRARY 8 Christians Brygge

This library houses one of the largest Jewish book collections in the world. Known as the Bibliotheca Judaica Simonseniana, it contains more than 50,000 volumes of Hebraica and Judaica, and hundreds of precious manuscripts, some dating from the 13th and 14th centuries.

MUSEUM OF THE DANISH RESISTANCE Esplanaden

This museum is devoted to the history and exploits of the Danish Resistance during World War II. The museum also features an exhibit of maps and photographs depicting the rescue of the Danish Jews from Hitler, their escape-route, their reception in Sweden and the welcome accorded them on their return to Denmark in 1945.

ISRAELSPLADS (ISRAEL SQUARE)

Located in the center of the city, this square was formerly known as "Green Square," since it had been for 200 years, the site of an open-air vegetable market. It was re-named Israel Square in 1968, on the 25th anniversary of the rescue of Danish Jews during the war. Its counterpart, in Jerusalem, is called "Denmark Square," a token of Israel's thanks to Scandinavia.'

JEWISH CEMETERY

On the Moellegade, is one of the oldest Jewish cemeteries in northern Europe. The earliest of its 5500 well-preserved tombstones marks the grave of David Israel, an early Jewish settler from Hamburg, Germany, who died in Denmark in 1693.

SYNAGOGUES

Copenhagen Great Synagogue *12 Krystalgade*
Hornbaek Synagogue *Granvej 7 #20-07-31*
Machzike Hadass *12 Ole Suhrsgade #12-77-99*

MIKVEH

Copenhagen *6 Ny Kongensgade #12-88-68. (The mikveh is housed in the Jewish Community Center, which also contains a small museum and library.)*

KOSHER PROVISIONS

Copenhagen *(restaurant) Rorholmsgade 2 #13-30-12*
(grocery) Vendersgade 16 #11-70-63 (kosher airline food boxes)
(grocery) 5 Classengade #42-09-81 (kosher airline food boxes)

AMERICAN EXPRESS OFFICE

Copenhagen *Amagertorv 18 (Stroget) #12-23-01*

YOUTH HOSTELS

Copenhagen *Herbergvejen 8 #28-97-15*
Sjaellandsbroen 55 #21-16-40

RAILROAD TIMETABLES

Copenhagen to:

Amsterdam	10.10—21.32
Berlin	10.12—20.35
Frankfurt	7.20—17.31
Helsinki	8.19—9.00 (next day)
London	9.25—9.14
Milan	7.20—5.25
Oslo	9.34—19.31
Paris	8.19—16.47
Vienna	13.10—9.50

Sweden

In 1774, the enlightened King Gustav III, revoked anti-Jewish ordinances of his predecessors and invited Jewish settlement. Jews settled in Stockholm, Gothenburg, Malmö, Norrkoping, Lund, and Uppsala. It was not until 1870 that Sweden's Jews achieved complete political emancipation and basic acceptance as citizens and members of the community. Sweden has the largest Jewish community in Scandinavia, with a Jewish population of 16,000.

GOTHENBURG

GREAT SYNAGOGUE Ostra Larmgatan 12

The oldest existing synagogue building in Sweden was constructed in 1855. The community itself dates from 1780. Adjoining this Liberal synagogue is the Jewish community center, which houses a kosher restaurant, religious school, and a small chapel used by Orthodox worshippers for daily services.

MALMÖ

SYNAGOGUE Foreningsgatan & Betianaplan

It was in this seventy-year-old synagogue that the last Jewish refugees from Denmark arrived, on Yom Kippur eve, in 1943, in time to join the congregation in the traditional *Kol Nidre* service.

JEWISH COMMUNITY CENTER Kamrergatan 11

This community center houses a home for the aged, mikveh, library, and youth facilities. For further information call 11-84-60.

STOCKHOLM

NIKOLAI POLISSTATION 19 Sjalagardsgatan

Now a police station, this building was originally Stockholm's first synagogue. The women's gallery is still intact.

GREAT SYNAGOGUE Wahrendorffsgatan 3

The Great Synagogue is the largest in the country. It was built in 1870 and designed by the Swedish architect Frederik Vilhelm Scholander. It is an oblong structure with galleries and a sky-lighted flat ceiling, instead of vaults. The large, tall windows in the aisles and in the galleries admit ample daylight. Triangular window-heads take the place of pointed arches. Still of medieval inspiration are the rose window and the bracketed cornice; but the overall impression is one of efficiency and concern for space and light. The decoration of the gallery parapet anticipates the freer design of the English Arts and Crafts movement of the 1880s.

JUDAICA HOUSE Nybrogatan 19

The Judaica House incorporates a Jewish community center, a Hebrew school, library, kosher dairy cafeteria, gymnasium, and meeting rooms. For further information call 63-65-66.

SYNAGOGUES

Gothenburg *Andra Langgatan 6*
(Liberal) Ostra Larmgatan 12 #13-67-78

Malmö *Foreningsgatan & Betianaplan*

Stockholm Great Synagogue *Wahrendorffsgatan 3 #23-51-60*
Adas Jeshurun *Nybrogatan 15 #61-82-82*
Adas Yisroel *St.Paulsgatan*

MIKVEH

Malmö *Kamrergatan 11 #11-84-60*

KOSHER PROVISIONS

Gothenburg *Larmgatan 12 #13-67-78*
(butcher) Stampgatan 68 #15-55-49

Malmö *(grocery) Carl Herslowsgatan #23-55-15*
(butcher) Skolgatan 2 #97-68-00

Stockholm *Nybrogatan 19 #63-65-66*
(grocery) Tjarhusgatan 5 #42-80-30
(restaurant) Vastgotagatan 16 #44-87-50

AMERICAN EXRESS OFFICES

Gothenburg *Ostra Hamngan 39 #17-40-20*

Malmö *Baltzarsgatan 6 #10-01-10*

Stockholm *Birger Jarisgatan 32 #24-09-80*

YOUTH HOSTELS

Gothenburg *Mejerigatan 2 #40-10-50*
Vastergotland #44-61-63

Malmö *Backavagen 18 #82-220*

Stockholm *Pipmakargrand 2 #68-57-86*
Drottningratan 15 #74-78-288

RAILROAD TIMETABLES

Stockholm to:

Amsterdam	11.13—9.54
Copenhagen	7.13—15.21
Frankfurt	15.13—12.31
Oslo	7.00—13.25
Paris	7.13—8.38 (next day)
Trondheim	7.45—22.05
Vienna	15.13—21.28 (next day)

Finland

Finland's first Jewish settlers came to the country in 1830—against their will! They were the so-called Cantonists or "Nicolaievskis," young Jewish boys, between the ages of 12 and 25 years, who had been drafted into the Russian army for a period of 25 years, and who were assigned to garrison duty in remote outposts of the Czarist empire, such as Finland and Siberia. The harsh conscription law had been designed in the reign of Czar Nicholas I, as a means of alienating the Cantonist (Jewish) child recruits from their own people and their religion and forcing their conversion to the Russian Orthodox Church. Each Jewish community within the Pale of settlement was assigned its quota of young draftees. There were special Jewish officers who carried out this task. They were known in Yiddish as *"chahpers,"* or kidnappers. These were the boys who would become, twenty-five years later, the first Jewish settlers in Finland. Assigned to garrison duty in Helsinki or Viipuri, on the Russian border, many chose to stay in Finland when their quarter-century of service had ended.

Until Finland gained its independence in 1917, the Jews were subjected to severe restrictions, limiting their places of residence, curtailing their freedom of movement, and narrowing the occupations open to them to such enterprises as the peddling of second-hand clothes.

During the Russo-Finnish War in 1939, virtually every able-bodied Jew enlisted in the Finnish army. Although Finland became an ally of Nazi Germany in 1941, she refused the Nazi's request to turn over to them the German-Jewish refugees and resisted all anti-Jewish measures. Some Jews in the Finnish army were, for a time, actually part of the German army on the Finnish-Russian border.

There are today about 1300 Jews in Finland.

HELSINKI

SYNAGOGUE Malminkatu 26

The only synagogue in the city was built in 1906. Preserved in a glass case, there is a wreath presented to the congregation on the occasion of a visit by Field Marshal Mannerheim, in 1944. The wreath memorializes the 23 Jewish soldiers who died in the Russo-Finnish War. (tel. 60-03-86)

AHVENANMAA (ALAND) ISLANDS

These islands, in the Gulf of Bothnia, contain the ruins of Bomarscund, a Russian fortress built partly by Jewish military conscripts. It was destroyed by British and French naval forces during the Crimean War in 1854. Nearby, are the graves of a number of Russian-Jewish soldiers.

KOSHER PROVISIONS

Helsinki *(grocery) Malminkatu 36 #694-16-51. (Open Wednesday, Thursday, and Friday.) Rabbi Schwartz will be glad to assist Jewish travellers regarding kosher provisions. Call 694-23-24.*

AMERICAN EXPRESS OFFICES

Hango *Bulevardi 10 #86-821*

Helsinki *Eteleranta 16 #17-19-20*

Turku *Humalistonkatu 3 #33-71-11*

YOUTH HOSTELS

Helsinki *Pohj Stadiontie 3 #496-071*
Jamerantaival 7 #461-811

Turku *Linnankatu 38 #16578*

RAILROAD TIMETABLES

Helsinki to:

Copenhagen .... 7.32—8.21 (next day)
Gothenburg .... 7.02—5.00
Hamburg .... 7.32—15.01 (next day)
Oslo .... 7.32—7.55 (next day)
Stockholm .... 7.00—19.45

Norway

Norway was the last of the Scandinavian countries to permit Jewish settlement. Despite the liberal constitution of 1814, it was not until 1851 that the ban on Jewish immigration was finally lifted. Following the pogroms in Russia in the 1880s, Jewish communities were organized in Oslo in 1892 and in Trondheim in 1905. There are about 950 Jews living in Norway.

OSLO

The synagogue built in 1920 was spared by the Nazis during their occupation of Norway. The Jewish Community Center is located at Bergstein 13. For further information call 46-94-18.

TRONDHEIM

The synagogue at Arkitekt Christiesgatan is the most northerly in the world, only three degrees below the Arctic Circle! It was originally built as Trondheim's main railroad station. During the war, the building was used by the Nazis as a warehouse and barracks. Its interior was desecrated, but has been restored following the war. A community center was added to the structure in 1955.

Sabbath candle-lighting time varies by many hours as the seasons change in this part of the world known as "land of the midnight sun." In the winter, the Sabbath candles are lit as early as 2.00 p.m., when the sun has already set. During the long days of mid-summer, the candles are lit as late as 11.00 p.m., when the rays of the sun are still high in the sky. In some parts of Scandinavia, there are as many as 22 days of daylight during the summer months. For further information about the Jewish community and when to light the Sabbath candles in this region, call 29-434.

KOSHER PROVISION

Oslo *(butcher)* *Stenberg Gate 19* *#46-82-15*

AMERICAN EXPRESS OFFICES

Bergen *Stradgt 5* *#32-10-80*

Oslo *Karl Johans Gate 33* *#42-91-50*

Stavanger *14 Kirkegatan* *#30-020*

Tromso *Frederik Langes Gt. 19/21* *#85-035*

Trondheim *Olav Tryggvassons Gt. 30* *#33-000*

YOUTH HOSTELS

Bergen *Montana Uh (Landas) #29-29-00*

Oslo *Haraldsheimvn 4 #22-29-65*
Trondheimsvn 271 #64-87-87

Trondheim *Weidemannsvei 41 #30-490*

RAILROAD TIMETABLES

Oslo to:

Amsterdam	11.00—9.54
Copenhagen	7.40—17.05
Hamburg	7.40—23.03
Helsinki	8.40—9.00 (next day)
Stockholm	8.40—15.00
Trondheim	8.00—14.38

Great Britain

Jewish settlement in England was encouraged by William the Conqueror during his reign (1066-1089). The Jews were permitted only to be moneylenders. They did not live in ghettos but rather congregated in certain streets—one of which was generally called "the Jewry"—close to a place of royal protection. Next to the king, Aaron the Jew from Lincoln, was the wealthiest Jew in England of his day. He was the head of a chain of moneylending offices and provided the funds that built the great cathedrals of Lincoln and Peterborough. During the first two centuries of Jewish settlement in England, there had been periods of reasonable security. The Jews were free to travel and enjoyed a large measure of communal autonomy. Starting in the 12th century, there were accusations of ritual murders, persecution, and even massacres of Jews. This culminated with the edict of Edward I, dated July 18, 1290, which expelled all Jews from England. The decree took effect on All Saints' Day of 1290. Some 3,000 Jews were driven from British soil, and would not return officially for over 365 years.

The Inquisition in Spain and Portugal in the end of the 14th century created the Marrano—a secret Jew, who practiced Catholicism in public but worshipped the Jewish faith in private. Many Marranos came to England during the 15th and 16th centuries, but did not reveal their true identity until 1656, when Oliver Cromwell permitted Jews to officially resettle in England. Cromwell was influenced by Menasseh ben Israel, the chief rabbi

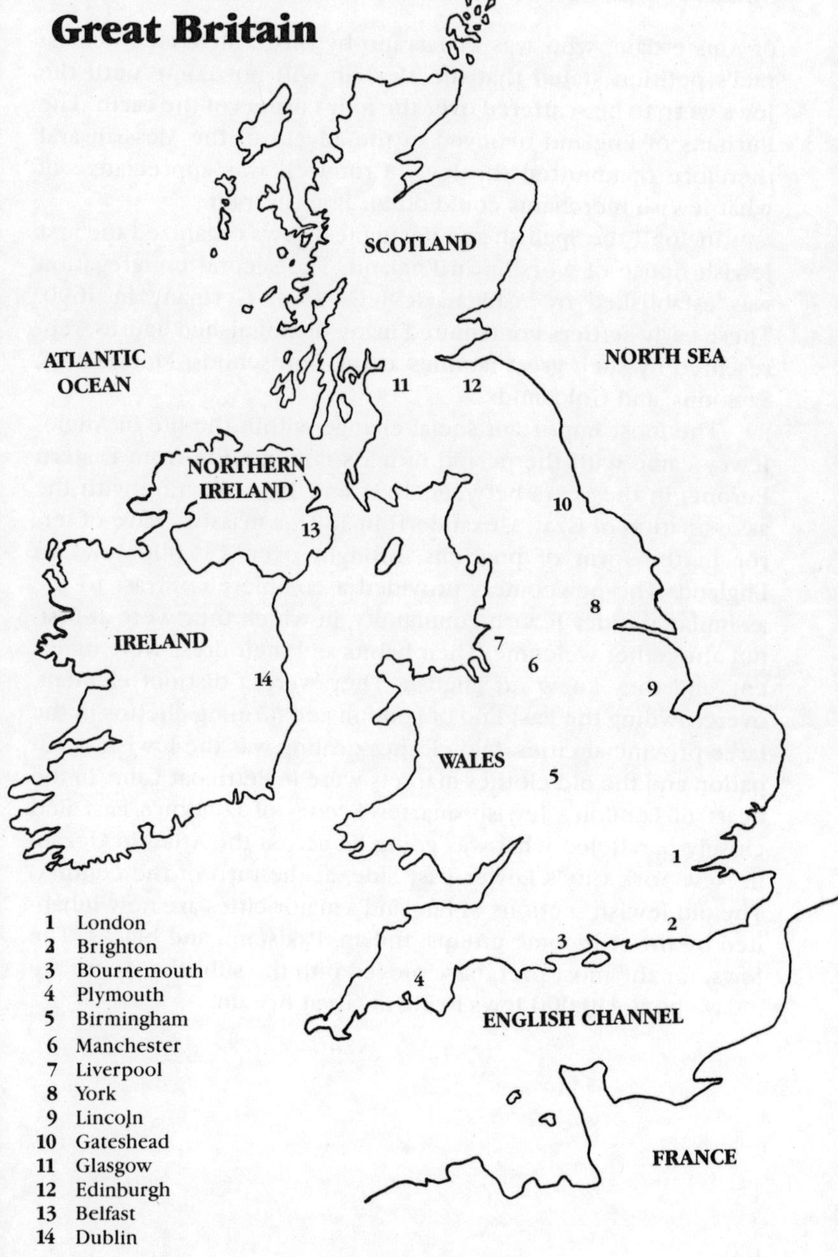

Great Britain
SCOTLAND
ATLANTIC OCEAN
NORTH SEA
11
12
NORTHERN IRELAND
10
13
8
IRELAND
7
6
14
9
WALES
5
1
2
3
4
ENGLISH CHANNEL
FRANCE
1 London
2 Brighton
3 Bournemouth
4 Plymouth
5 Birmingham
6 Manchester
7 Liverpool
8 York
9 Lincoln
10 Gateshead
11 Glasgow
12 Edinburgh
13 Belfast
14 Dublin

of Amsterdam, who was a Marrano by birth. Menasseh ben Israel's petition stated that the Messiah will not come until the Jews were to be scattered over the four corners of the earth. The Puritans of England believed in the advent of the Messiah and therefore re-admitted the Jews. Cromwell was appreciative of what Jewish merchants could do for English trade.

In 1657, the Spanish and Portuguese Jews organized the first Jewish house of worship in England. The second congregation was established by Ashkenazic Jews from Germany in 1690. These early settlers contributed many distinguished figures, represented by such great families as the Rothschilds, Montefiores, Sassoons, and Goldsmids.

The most important social change within the life of Anglo-Jewry came with the period of mass immigration from Eastern Europe, in the years between 1881 and 1914. Starting with the assassination of Czar AlexanderII in 1881, a massive wave of terror in the form of pogroms, brought over 235,000 Jews to England. The newcomers provided a complete contrast to the assimilated older Jewish community, in which they were at first, not altogether welcome. Their habits and their dress were different, and they knew no English. They were a distinct element, overcrowding the East End of London and forming ghettos in the large provincial cities. Old clothes dealing was the Jewish occupation and the old clothes markets were in Petticoat Lane, in the heart of London's Jewish quarter. Scenes of London's East End closely paralleled what was going on across the Atlantic Ocean, in New York City's Lower East Side, at the turn of the century. The old Jewish sections of England's major cities are now inhabited by lower-income groups: Indian, Pakistani, and blacks. The Jews, for the most part, have moved into the suburbs. There are today about 410,000 Jews living in Great Britain.

BRIGHTON

HEBREW CONGREGATION Middle Street

Built in 1874 by architect Thomas Lainson, the Hebrew Congregation of Brighton was designed as a private synagogue for the family of Albert Sassoon. Sassoon was a member of the noted family of industrialists, traders, statesmen, poets, and entrepreneurs. The synagogue is dominated by its exquisite brass furnishings. The ark is enclosed by two brass gates, appearing as a gilded cage.

The Bombay Bar (St. George's Road and Paston Place) was the mausoleum of Albert Sassoon and his son. The remains were removed in 1933.

LINCOLN

There are three buildings of Norman design which are believed to be pre-Expulsion homes of Jews. One house is said to belong to Aaron the Jew of Lincoln, who was one of the wealthiest men in England. He owned a chain of money-lending offices, which provided funds for the construction of the cathedrals of Lincoln and Peterborough.

Another building is said to have been the synagogue. These houses are located on the hillside of Steep Hill, just below the ancient cathedral.

In 1255, an eight-year-old named "Hugh" was found dead. The Jews of Lincoln were accused of murdering for ritual purposes. This touched off massacres of Jews throughout England. The tomb of "Little St. Hugh" is located in the south aisle of the Lincoln Cathedral.

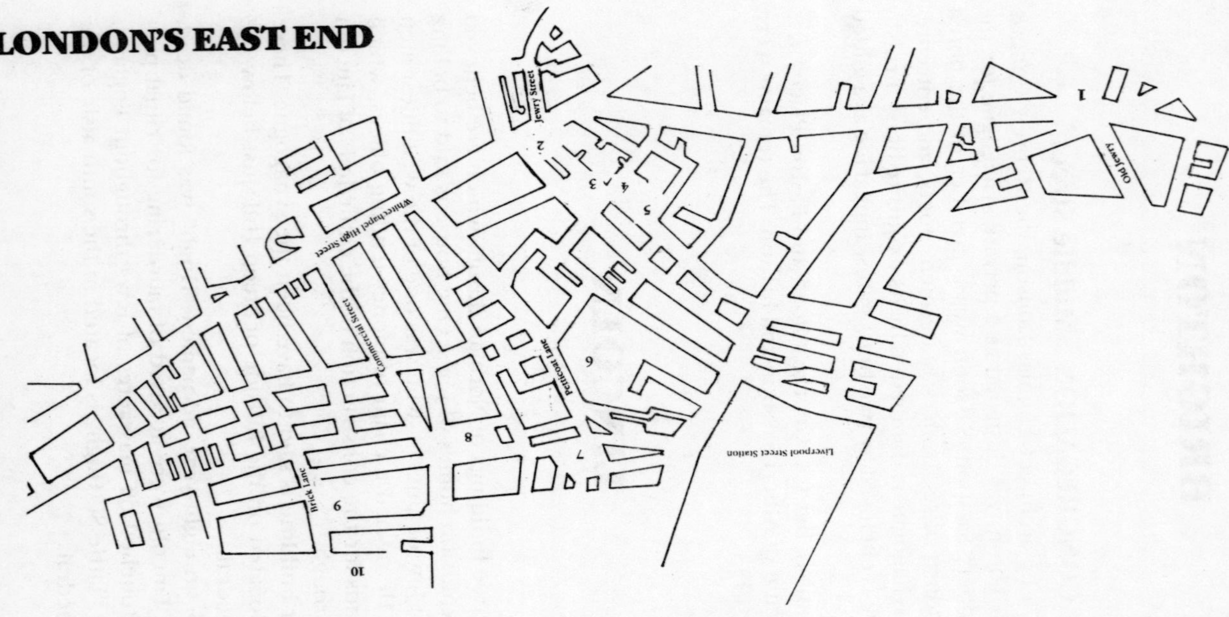
LONDON'S EAST END
Old Jewry
Jewry Street
Whitechapel High Street
Commercial Street
Petticoat Lane
Brick Lane
Liverpool Street Station
1
2
3
4
5
6
7
8
9
10
1 Old Jewry
2 Jewry Street
3 Site of the Great Synagogue
4 Site of First Synagogue in England
5 Bevis Marks Synagogue
6 Petticoat Lane
7 Sandy's Road Synagogue
8 Soup Kitchen for the Jewish Poor
9 Former Machzikei Hadass Synagogue
10 Former Princelet Street Shul

LONDON

(London Underground Stations in italics)

OLD JEWRY

Bank Station (Northern Line)

This small street, just off Poultry Street, was once the heart of the pre-Expulsion Jewish community.

JEWRY

Aldgate Station (Circle Line)

This was the center of the Jewish community in pre-Expulsion London, after they were forced to move from Old Jewry because of anti-Semitic riots, at the time of Richard I's coronation.

SITE OF DUKE'S PLACE SYNAGOGUE

Aldgate Station (Circle Line)

The Great Synagogue of London, the Duke's Place Shul, was the mother congregation of the Ashkenazic Jews and was organized in 1690. The synagogue which stood at this location was built in 1790 and was designed by architect James Spillar. The Neoclassical building seated 750 people, was *the* synagogue of British Jewry where all of the community's major celebrations took place. In May, 1941, the Great Synagogue was bombed by the Nazis during the Blitzkrieg over London. Today, all that remains of the Great Synagogue is an historic plaque.

SITE OF FIRST SYNAGOGUE—AFTER THE RESETTLEMENT

Aldgate Station (Circle Line)

The first Jewish house of worship after the Resettlement of the Jews in England was opened in 1657, in the upper floor of a house in Creechurch Lane, which is located at the corner of Bury Street, at the base of the Cunard Line Building. This historic plaque is located just around the corner from the Bevis Marks Synagogue.

BEVIS MARKS SYNAGOGUE—CONGREGATION SHAAR HASHOMAYIM 4 Heneage Lane

Aldgate Station (Circle Line)

The oldest in England, the Bevis Marks, Spanish and Portuguese Synagogue, was organized in 1657. Its first location was at Creechurch Lane and Bury Street, just around the corner from the present building. This Sephardic congregation modelled its synagogue after the Great Synagogue (esnoga) of Amsterdam. It was designed in 1701 by master-builder, Joseph Avis. Mr. Avis, a Quaker, refused to accept the overpayment of the construction costs for this house of worship. It is said that Queen Anne presented an oak beam from one of the royal navy's ships, to be incorporated in the roof of the building. The Bevis Marks Syn-

Historic plaque in London's East End.

Exterior view of the Bevis Marks Synagogue.

agogue measures 80 feet x 50 feet. The magnificent wooden ark, resembling a reredos, is built in the classical architectural style, in the manner of Sir Christopher Wren's time. There are seven great hanging many-branched candelabra, which are still used to light the building with candlelight on Sabbaths, Festivals and during wedding ceremonies. The seven represent the days of the week. There are ten brass candlesticks before the ark, symbolizing the Ten Commandments. There are twelve columns supporting the women's gallery, representing the twelve tribes of Israel.

There are morning services at the Bevis Marks Synagogue at 7.30 a.m. (Monday, Thursday, and Saturday).

Recently, the congregation was having financial difficulties. The Board of Directors of the congregation decided to sell a parcel of land in front of the historic synagogue building. Today, there is a four-story office building standing in front of the old Bevis Marks Synagogue. Part of the original 1701 limestone portal with the congregation's entablature, engraved in Hebrew, has been incorporated into the modern office building's facade.

PETTICOAT LANE

The East End of London was similar to New York City's Lower East Side at the turn of the century. It was the first home for thousands of Jewish refugees, fleeing the pogroms of Eastern Europe after 1881. Most were unskilled laborers, so they worked in

Interior view of the Bevis Marks Synagogue.

the garment industries. Many peddled old clothing in the market in Petticoat Lane, which was the heart of London's Jewish quarter. Sunday mornings are still active as the "street market." Some of the old Yiddish-speaking merchants have been replaced with the newer immigrants—from India and Pakistan. Wentworth Street is the weekday marketplace.

FORMER SYNAGOGUE 48a Artillery Lane

The building housing the "Cosmart House—Felas Farms," was originally built as a synagogue around the turn of the century. Notice the cupola above the roof.

SANDY'S ROW SHUL

At the corner of Artillery Lane and Sandy's Row stands one of the few remaining synagogues in London's East End. It was built in 1854 and there are still weekly Sabbath services.

SOUP KITCHENS Brune Street

In order to feed the masses of Jewish poor, following the major wave of immigration around the turn of the century, the Jewish relief agencies set up soup kitchens. The one located on Brune Street was built in 1902. The engraved entablature reads,"Soup Kitchen for the Jewish Poor." The doors on the right are marked, "way in" and the doors on the left read, "way out."

FORMER SYNAGOGUE 19 Princelet Street

A tenement-style synagogue, similar to the ones found in New York City's Lower East Side, today stands abandoned. If you peek through the keyhole, you can see the old ark and bimah. There was a women's gallery upstairs.

FORMER MACHZIKEI HADASS SYNAGOGUE 59 Brick Lane (corner Fournier Street)

Built in 1763 as a Huguenot (French) church, the building, for many years, housed the Jewish congregation, Machzikei Hadass. It was recently purchased by the local Pakistani groups and is now used as a mosque. Notice the entablature with the Ten Com-

Soup kitchen for the Jewish poor in London's East End.

mandment tablets and the Latin inscription below, along the Fournier Street facade.

FORMER SYNAGOGUE 2b Heneage Street

Just east of Brick Lane stands a former synagogue. It is presently used as a food market, specializing in Indian and Pakistani foods. As you enter the shop, you can see what, at one time, was the women's balcony.

OTHER FORMER SYNAGOGUES

There are several abandoned synagogues in the East End of London and in the vicinity of Whitechapel, Spitafields, Stepney Green, Mile End, and West Ham. These areas have been designated as Urban Renewal districts. Many of these old synagogue buildings may be demolished in the very near future. Below is a partial list of the locations of old synagogues:

- Whitechapel Road & Old Castle Street
- Alie Street & Leman Street
- Old Montague Street & Mount Hope Street
- Deal Street & Chicksand Stret
- Thrawl Street (Etz Chaim Yeshiva)

SITE OF JEWS FREE SCHOOL Aldgate Street

This school, sponsored by the Jewish relief agencies, was located near the Brune Street soup kitchen. The remains of the bombed-out building now house shops and warehouses. The Jews Free School was located between Frying Pan Alley, Bell Lane, and Middlesex Street.

SITE OF THE PUBLIC BATHS Old Castle Street (near Whitechapel Street)

Many of the tenements which housed the poor Jewish immigrants, at the turn of the century, did not have running hot water. They were similar to the "cold water flats" of New York City's Lower East Side. The immigrants would therefore go to the public baths for their weekly scrub-down.

SITE OF THE JEWS' TEMPORARY SHELTER 63 Mansell St.

This was the place where thousands of newly-arrived Jewish immigrants from Eastern Europe found temporary shelter, between the years 1881 and 1914.

JEWISH HOSPITAL

Stepney Green Station (District Line)

JEWISH MATERNITY HOSPITAL

Whitechapel Station (Metropolitan Line)

JEWISH CEMETERIES

Mile End Station (District Line)

The oldest Jewish cemetery (Beth Haim Velho) is situated behind the Sephardic Home for the Aged, at 253 Mile End Road. It is the first Resettlement cemetery and was acquired in 1657. Such personalities as Abraham Fernandez Carvajal, regarded as the founder of the modern Anglo-Jewish community, Haham David Nieto, a great Sephardic leader, and Dr.Fernando Mendes, the physician who attended Charles II at his deathbed, are buried here. This cemetery is open to the public.

The second oldest Jewish cemetery is located at Alderney Road (Stepney Green Station—District Line). It was opened in 1696 by the Ashkenazic organizers of the Duke's Place Synagogue. This cemetery is not open to the public.

The Beth Haim Novo is located at 329 Mile End Road. It is the third oldest Jewish cemetery in England. It was first used in 1733 by the Sephardic community. It is not open to the public.

BRITISH MUSEUM Great Russel Street

Tottenham Courtern Road Station (Northern Line)

The British Museum and British Library house one of the world's largest collections of Judaica. There are Torah scrolls from the now vanished Jewish community in Kai-Feng Fu, in China, illuminated Bibles and haggadahs, and priceless artifacts.

JEWISH MUSEUM Upper Woburn Place (Woburn House)

Euston Station (Victoria Line)

As you enter the building be prepared to undergo a security

check. This building houses British Jewry's principle communal organizations. It houses the United Synagogue, the Board of Deputies, the Chief Rabbi's office, and the court of the London Beth Din.

The Jewish Museum was opened in 1932. It houses ritual objects from old synagogues in London and throughout Europe. Some items of note are: a Staffordshire jug, depicting the boxing fight between a Sephardic Jew, Daniel Mendoza, and Richard Humphreys, in 1789. Mendoza defeated the previous champion and turned boxing into an art and was known as the "father of modern boxing." There is a large gilded ark, which was discovered by a bookseller attending an auction sale at Chillingham Castle in Northumberland, where it had been used as a wardrobe in a servant's room. It was duly purchased and when restored, was found to date from the 16th century and to be of Italian origin, probably from a Venetian synagogue.

Museum hours: Tues. - Thur. (Fri. in summer) 10-4 p.m.
Sun. (Fri. in winter) 10 - 12.45 p.m. tel. # (01) 388-4525

MARBLE ARCH SYNAGOGUE
32 Great Cumberland Place

Marble Arch Station (Central Line)

This is the second home of the historic Great Synagogue on Duke's Place. The Duke's Place Synagogue was founded in 1690 by Ashkenazic Jews and was *the* synagogue of British Jewry, where all the community's major celebrations took place. It was built in 1790 but was destroyed by Nazi bombing raids in World War II. The present synagogue is not an independent or free-standing structure but is rather housed in a luxury housing complex near Marble Arch.

WEST LONDON SYNAGOGUE
34 Upper Berkeley Street

Edgeware Road Station (District Line)

Designed in 1870 by the architectural firm of Davis and Emanuel, the West London Synagogue is one of the most glorious synagogue structures in England. It was organized in 1842 as a break from the Sephardic Bevis Marks Synagogue. It was founded by the most prominent Jewish families in London—the Mocattas, Henriqueses, Montefiores, and the Goldsmids. The most luxurious materials were incorporated in the synagogue's design including marble columns and floor tiles, mahogany paneling, and leather seats. The stained-glass windows depict exquisite floral patterns. The congregation follows the Reform ritual, which is similar to the Conservative Movement in the United States (the Liberal Movement in Europe is similar to the Reform Movement in the United States). The congregation consists of 2500 families.

STAMFORD HILL

This section, north of London, is the Chassidic Section. There are many small synagogues (*shteeblech*) as well as many yeshivas. There are some Persian and Indian synagogues in this area as well.

Other Jewish sections of London are in Golders Green, Henden, Finchley, and Edgware.

WESTMINSTER SYNAGOGUE (tel. (01) 584-3953)
Rutlands Gardens, Knightsbridge S.W.7

The 1564 Torah scrolls confiscated by the Nazis and stored in Prague, Czechoslovakia during World War II were shipped to this synagogue in 1964. The Westminster Synagogue, the former residence of Queen Victoria's father, the Duke of Kent, has repaired many of these Torah scrolls and has shipped them to Jewish communities throughout the world. The Torah scrolls not on permanent loan to needy Jewish communities are on display in the Westminster Synagogue.

MANCHESTER

SPANISH AND PORTUGUESE SYNAGOGUE
190 Cheetham Hill Road

Located in the old section of Manchester, the old Spanish & Portuguese Synagogue has just recently become an historic landmark and Jewish Museum (tel. #(061) 834-9879). Its cornerstone was laid in 1873 by Sir Albert Sassoon. To the right of the museum stand several former synagogue structures; United Synagogue (housed in a former church), the Great Synagogue (at #159) was built in 1857 but now stands in ruins, and the former New Synagogue & Beth Hamedrash, which still displays a Star of David (now occupied by Simon & Simon Lamp Factory).

GLASGOW, SCOTLAND

GARNETHILL SYNAGOGUE 29 Garnethill Street

Overlooking the city of Glasgow is the most elegant synagogue in Scotland. Built in 1879 by architect Sir John McEwen, the synagogue resembles the West London Synagogue. The ark is recessed into a skylighted apse. There are exquisite marble columns and floor tiles. The stained-glass windows depict beautiful floral patterns. Sir Issac Wolfson, the first Jew in Scotland to be made a peer and Sir Maurice Bloch, whiskey-maker and philanthropist, were members of this synagogue. The synagogue is used on the Sabbath and for special occasions only. The present Jewish community is located in the suburban community of Giffnock.

The largest manufacturer of kilts is Denis Bonchy Cohen, of Glasgow.

YORK

CLIFFORD'S TOWER

The Third Crusade inflamed the Christians against the "infidel" Jews in their midst. Debtors seized the occasion of the current anti-Jewish feeling to cause riots and to burn the records of transactions in which they were involved. The Jews fled into Clifford's Tower, the central tower of a medieval castle, built on a Norman mound. When the angry mobs broke into the tower, they found that many of the Jews had committed suicide.Those remaining alive were slaughtered on the spot. Yom Tov of Joigny, an eminent scholar from France, was living in York in 1190, and was among the Jews who committed suicide during the Festival of Passover, in Clifford's Tower. The tower is still there, but it is now a stone ruin.

Interior view of the Garnethill Synagogue of Glasgow, Scotland.

SYNAGOGUES

England

Birmingham *Ellis Street #643-0884*
133 Pershore Road #440-4044
11 Park Road
(Progressive) 4 Sheepcote Street #643-5640

Blackburn *19 Clayton Street #53834*

Blackpool *Leamington Road #28614*
(Reform) Raikes Pde. #32513

Bolton *Central Street*

Bournemouth *Wooton Gardens #27433*
(Reform) 53 Christchurch Road #34451

Bradford *Springhurst Road #499-979*
(Reform) Manningham Lane #28925

Brighton *66 Middle Street #27785*

Bristol *9 Park Row #23538*
(Progressive) 43 Bannerman Road #541-937

Bromley *28 Highland Road #460-5460*

Cambridge *Ellis Court & Thompson Lane*

Chatham *High Street*

Cheltenham *St. Jame's Square*

Chingford *Marborough Road*

Colchester *Priory Street*

Coventry *Barras Lane #20168*

Crawley *(Progressive) Langley Lane*

Croydon *30 Elmont Road #684-4726*

Derby *270 Burton Road*

Eastbourne *22 Susans Road*

Epsom *Prospect Place #21150*

Gateshead *180 Bewick Road #71338*

Greenford *39 Lodfield Lane*

Grimsby *Heneage Road*

Harlow *Harnert's Road*

Harold Hill *Trowbridge Road*

Harrogate *St. Mary's Walk*

Hove *29 New Church Road*
Holland Road
(Liberal) 6 Lansdown Road
(Reform) Palmeira Avenue

Hull *Osborne Street*
Park Street
Linnaeus Street #228-252

Leeds *21 Newton Park View #624-191*
46 Spencer Place #33304
1 Louis Street #623-254
Winton Street
Reginald Terrace
(Reform) Roman Avenue #665-256
98 Chapeltown Road #621-351
Belgrave Street
Chapeltown Road & Moortown

Leicester *(Progressive) Highfield Street #832-927*

Letchworth *15 Sollershott East*

Liverpool *Princes Road #709-3431*
Greenbank Drive #733-1417
2 Dove Tale Road
(Liberal) Church Road North 15 #733-5871
101 Ullet Road
Mather Avenue #427-6848
Dunbabi Road #722-2079

London

There are several hundred synagogues throughout the metropolitan London area. For information regarding services and locations of synagogues you may contact any of the following organizations;

United Synagogue tel. (01) 387-4300
Federation of Synagogues tel. (01) 247-4471
Union of Orthodox Hebrew Congregations tel. (01) 802-6226
Spanish & Portuguese Jews' Congregation tel. (01) 289-2573
Liberal Synagogues tel. (01) 580-1663
Reform Synagogues tel. (01) 349-4731

Luton *116 Bury Park Road #25032*

Manchester *Cheltenham Cres. #792-1233*
Upper Park Road #740-3905

Sunnybank Road #766-7442
Leicester Road #740-4830
453 Cheethan Hill Road #740-7788
18 Moor Lane #773-1344
Shay Lane #980-6549
Middleton Road #740-4766
Bury Old Road #740-1210
Ribble Drive #766-5986
62 Singleton Road #740-1629
17 North Comberland Street #792-1313
Stenecourt & Holden Road #740-4027
Vine Street #792-4258
132 Leicester Road #792-2413
Bury New Road #773-1978
14 Hesketh Road #973-2172
Parkview Road #773-6092
Old Lansdowne Road #445-5731
Wilbraham Road #224-1366
Meade Hill #740-9586
Park Lane #766-3732
8 Queenston Road #445-1943
Coniston Road #428-8242

REFORM
Atrinchan Road #980-7595
Jackson's Row #834-0415
Elms Street #796-5063

Margate *Godwin Road #20964*
Middlesborough *Park Road South #819590*
Newcastle *Great North Road*
37 Eskdale Terrace
Graham Park Road
(Reform) Clayton Road #842502

Northampton *Overstone Road*

Norwich *3a Earlham Road #23948*

Nottingham *Shakespeare Street* *#42004*
(Progressive) *Lloyd Street* *#325111*

Oxford *21 Richmond Road* *#53042*

Peterborough *142 Cobden Avenue* *#71282*

Plymouth *Catherine Street* *#661626*

Portsmouth *The Thicket* *#824391*

Ramsgate *Hereson Road*

Reading *Goldsmith Road* *#53954*

Romford *25 Eastern Road*

Ruislip *Shenley Avenue* *#32934*

St. Albans *Oswald Road* *#54872*

St. Annes *Orchard Road* *#721831*

Sale *14 Hesketh Road* *#2172*

Sheffield *Wilson Road* *#360299*
127 Psalter Lane *#52296*

Solihull *3 Manestary Drive*

Southampton *Mordaunt Road* *#773647*

Southend *Finchley Road*
(Reform) *851 London Road* *#76349*

South Shields *25 Beach Road* *#84508*

Stoke *Birch Terrace* *#641116*

Sunderland *Ryhope Road* *#658093*
Monbray Road *#57417*

Sutton *14 Cedar Road* *#8029*

Torquay *Abbey Road* *#605352*

Watford *16 Nascot Road* *#22755*

Whitley Bay *2 Oxford Street* *#521367*

Wolverhampton *Fryer Street*

York *#791703*

Northern Ireland

Belfast *49 Somerton Road #777974*

Scotland

Aberdee *74 Dee Street #22135*

Dundee *St. Mary Place #28140*

Edinburgh *4 Salisbury Road #667-3144*

Glasgow *20 Belleisle Street #634-2001*
29 Garnet Street #332-4151
Maryville Avenue #638-6600
125 Niddrie Road #423-4062
Clarkson Road #644-3611
(Reform) 147 Ayr Road #639-4083
Beech Avenue #639-2442
Faloch Road #632-5025

Wales

Aberdare *19a Seymor Street #588-3586*

Cardiff *Cathedral Road*
Penylan & Brandreth Roads #483959
(Reform) Moira Terrace #691243

Llandudno *Church Walk #76848*

Merthry Tydfil *Church Street #3113*

Swansea *Ffynone Street #207146*

MIKVEHS

England

Birmingham Bourrnille Lane Baths *#440-1019*

Bournemouth *Wooton Gardens #27433*

Gateshead *180 Benwick Street #773-047*

Leeds *368 Harrogate Road #685119*

Leicester Highfield Street Synagogue *#700130*

Liverpool *Dundabin Road #722-2079*

Manchester *Broom Holme & Tetlow Lane #792-3970*
Sedgley Park Road #773-1537

Southport *Arnside Road #32964*

London *40 Queen Elizabeth Walk N16 #802-6226*

Westcliff *Genesta Road #44900*

Northern Ireland

Belfast *49 Somerton Road #777974*

Scotland

Glasgow *Maryville Avenue #638-6600*

Wales

Cardiff Wales Empire Pool Building *#22296*

KOSHER RESTAURANTS

England

Bournemouth Green Park Hotel *#34345*
New Ambassador Hotel #25453

Ilford *376 Crambrook Road #7097/2474*

London Bloom's *90 Whitechapel High Street (E1)*
#247-6835

Deli·King

Menorah Hotel *54 Clapton Common (E5) #806-4925*
Kadimah Hotel *146 Clapton Common (E5) #800-5960*

Aviv 87 High Street (Edgware) #(01) 952-2484

Kosherina 8-9 Sentinel Sguare (Hendon) #(01) 202-9870

Aviva Hotel *350 Finchley Road (NW3) #794-6756*

Pizza Pitta 119 Golders Green Road #(01) 455-8921

Bloom's *130 Golders Green Road (NW11) #455-1338*

Zacki's Restaurant *634 Finchley Road*
Reuben's Restaurant *20a Baker Street (W1) #935-5945*
Hillel House *1 Endsleigh Street (WC1H) #388-0802*

Gateshead *(bakery) 215 Coatsworth Road #77201*

Manchester
Fulda's Hotel *84 Bury Old Road #740-4551*

Deli King *Kings Road*

Scotland

Edinburgh *(bakery) 84 East Crosscauseway #667-1406*
(butcher) 30 Buccleuch Street #667-2421

Glasgow Freed's Restaurant *49 Coplaw Street #423-8911*
(grocery) 2 Burnfield Road #638-4383

NOTE: All (18) Grodzinski Bakeries throughout London are kosher. They also have ready-to-go sandwiches.

AMERICAN EXPRESS OFFICES

Ashford *26 Bank Street #34321*

Barrow *202 Dalton Road #25438*

Bedford *13 Mull Street #218221*

Birmingham *17 Martineau Square #233-2141*

Blackpool *314 Church Street #22331*

Bolton *9 Deansgate #34281*

Bradford *1 Duckworth Lane #491151*

Brighton *66 Churchill Square #21242*

Bristol *15 Colston Street #23031*

Broadstairs *52b High Street #65264*

Burton *71 High Street #217564*

Camborne *37 Trelowarren Street #714707*

Cambridge *25 Sidney Street #51636*

Chertsry *84 Guilford Street #61155*

Chestnut *7 Lynton Parade #38234*

Chester *8 Paddock Row #22797*

Eastbourne *29 Grove Road #22071*

Esher *64 High Street #63672*

Falmouth *48 Arwenwack Street #311000*

Fareham *187 West Street #232535*

Folkestone *98 Sandgate Road #51074*

Harpenden *3 Station Road #62222*

Harrogate *45 James Street #64144*

Helston *5 Wendron Road #3345*

Huddersfield *35 William Street #26666*

Hull *Paragon Street* *#25681*

Ickenham *5 Swakeleys Road* *#31313*

Ipswich *41 The Buttermarket* *#210821*

Lancaster *39a Penny Street* *#68451*

Leeds *60 Boar Lane* *#448911*

Little Chalfont *Nightingale Corner* *#4512*

Liverpool *54 Lord Stret* *#9202*

London *6 Haymarket* *#930-4411*
52 Cannon Street *#248-2671*
89 Mount Street *#499-4436*
78 Brompton Road *#584-6182*
147 Victoria Street *#828-7411*

Lutton *47 George Street* *#421-751*

Maidenhead *11 High Street* *#29777*

Manchester *1 Cross Street* *#833-0121*

Northampton *14 The Drapery* *#30261*

Nottingham *92 Upper Parliament Street* *#412310*

Oxford *37 Upper Barr* *#770841*

Reading *4 Yield Hall Place* *#580456*

Southampton *99 Above Bar* *#34722*

Stratford *5a Chapel Street* *#293582*

Northern Ireland

Belfast *23/31 Waring Street* *#230321*

Scotland

Aberdeen *193 Union Street* *#52734*

Glasgow *115 Hope Street* *#221-4366*

St. Andrews (Fife) *203 South Street* *#74451*

Wales

Cardiff *33 Oxford House* #44041

Swansea *2 Portland Street* #469214

YOUTH HOSTELS

England

Bath *Bathwick Hill* #65674

Brighton *Patcham Place* #556196

Bristol *Redland Green* #52753

Cambridge *97 Tenison Road* #354601

Canterbury *54 New Dover Road* #62911

Dover *306 London Road* #201314

Lincoln *77 South Park* #22076

London *36 Carter Lane (EC4V)* #236-4965
38 Bolton Gardens (SW5) #373-7083
4 Wellgarth Road (NW11) #458-9054
84 Highgate West Hill (N6) #340-1831

Norwich *112 Turner Road* #27647

Oxford *Jack Straw's Lane* #62997

Penzance *Castle Hormeck* #2666

Plymouth *Devonport Road* #52189

Portsmouth *Wymering Manor* #375661

Salisbury *Milford Hill House* #27572

Southampton *461 Winchester Road* #769607

Winchester *1 Water Lane* #53723

York *Haverford, Water End* #53147

RAILROAD TIMETABLES

London to:

Amsterdam	8.15—17.35
Belfast	10.30—22.25
Berlin	9.15—6.28
Copenhagen	9.15—9.17 (next day)
Glasgow	7.45—13.02
Paris	9.45—17.50
Rome	9.45—10.05 (next day)
Venice	9.45—7.14
Vienna	9.15—9.50 (next day)

Ireland

SYNAGOGUES

Cork *10 South Terrace #241091*

Dublin *Adelaide Road*
Dolphins Barn.
Leinster Road West 6
77 Terenure Road North
(Progressive) 7 Leicester Avenue

KOSHER PROVISIONS

Dublin *(butcher) 42 Lower Clansbrassil Street #753492*
(butcher) 35 Lower Clansbrassil Street #751865
(grocery) 84 Terenure Road North #907469

SABBATH CANDLELIGHTING TIMETABLES

This is a perpetual timetable. The Sabbath candles are lit in connection with the sunset. The sun will set at precisely the same time on January 1 every year. If January 1 is a Friday this year and Sabbath candles are lit at 16.27 in Zurich, next year, January 1 may not be on a Friday, so you would have to add a few extra minutes to the timetable and light Sabbath candles in Zurich for that week at 16.23

Amsterdam

	Begins	Ends
Sept 28	18.10	20.14
Oct 5	18.10	18.58
12	17.50	18.42
19	17.17	18.28
26	17.02	18.14
Nov 2	16.49	18.02
9	16.36	17.51
16	16.26	17.41
23	16.17	17.34
30	16.11	17.29
Dec 7	16.07	17.27
14	16.06	17.26
21	16.09	17.29
28	16.13	17.33
Jan 4	16.21	17.40
11	16.30	17.49
18	16.41	17.58
25	16.54	18.09
Feb 1	17.06	18.21
8	17.20	18.33
15	17.33	18.45
22	17.46	18.57
Mar 1	18.10	19.10
8	18.25	19.22
15	18.35	19.35
22	18.50	19.47
29	19.00	20.00
Apr 5	19.00	21.14
12	19.00	21.27
19	19.10	21.41
26	19.20	21.55
May 3	19.30	22.10
10	19.40	22.25
17	19.50	22.39
24	20.00	22.53
31	20.05	23.05
Jun 7	20.10	23.15
14	20.15	23.22
21	20.20	23.25
28	20.20	23.24

	Begins	Ends		Begins	Ends
Jul 5	20.15	23.20	16	19.25	22.01
12	20.15	23.12	23	19.25	21.44
19	20.05	23.01	30	19.05	21.27
26	20.00	22.48	Sep 6	18.55	21.09
Aug 2	19.50	22.33	13	18.40	20.52
9	19.40	22.18			

Copenhagen

Sep 28	17.30	19.40	29	18.15	19.35
Oct 5	17.00	18.25	Apr 5	18.30	19.50
12	17.00	18.05	12	18.45	21.05
19	16.45	17.55	19	18.45	21.15
26	16.42	17.50	26	19.00	21.35
Nov 2	16.15	17.20	May 3	19.00	21.50
9	16.00	17.15	10	19.15	22.10
16	17.00	16.55	17	19.30	22.25
23	15.45	16.50	24	19.45	22.45
30	15.45	16.45	31	20.00	22.55
Dec 7	15.45	16.40	Jun 7	20.00	23.05
14	15.17	16.44	14	20.00	23.05
21	15.45	16.35	21	20.00	23.05
28	15.40	16.35	28	20.00	23.05
Jan 4	15.45	16.40	Jul 5	20.00	23.00
11	15.45	16.50	12	20.00	22.55
18	16.00	17.00	19	19.45	22.45
25	16.15	17.10	26	19.30	22.30
Feb 1	16.30	17.40	Aug 2	19.15	22.15
8	17.00	17.55	9	19.00	22.00
15	17.00	18.10	16	18.45	21.40
22	17.10	18.25	23	18.30	21.25
Mar 1	17.30	18.35	30	18.15	21.05
8	17.45	18.50	Sep 6	18.00	20.45
15	18.00	19.05	13	18.00	20.25
22	18.00	19.20			

London

	Begins	Ends
Sep 28	18.24	19.34
Oct 5	18.09	19.34
12	17.53	19.03
19	17.38	18.48
26	17.24	18.35
Nov 2	16.11	17.23
9	15.59	17.12
16	15.49	17.04
23	15.41	16.57
30	15.35	16.52
Dec 7	15.32	16.49
14	15.31	16.49
21	15.33	16.52
28	15.38	16.56
Jan 4	15.45	17.03
11	15.54	17.11
18	16.05	17.21
25	16.17	17.31
Feb 1	16.30	17.43
8	16.42	17.54
15	16.55	18.06
22	17.08	18.18
Mar 1	17.20	18.30
8	17.32	18.42
15	17.45	18.54
22	17.56	19.06
29	18.08	19.18
Apr 5	19.20	20.31
12	19.32	20.44
19	19.43	20.58
26	19.55	21.11
May 3	20.06	21.25
10	20.18	21.39
17	20.28	21.53
24	20.38	22.06
31	20.47	22.17
Jun 7	20.54	22.26
14	20.58	22.33
21	21.01	22.36
28	21.01	22.35
Jul 5	20.59	22.31
12	20.54	22.24
19	20.47	22.14
26	20.38	22.02
Aug 2	20.27	21.48
9	20.14	21.33
16	20.01	21.17
23	19.46	21.00
30	19.31	20.44

NOTE: On June 21, the longest Sabbath of the year, in Glasgow, Scotland, Sabbath begins at 21.51 and ends at 23.47.

Paris

Sep 28	19.16	20.23
Oct 5	18.02	19.08
12	17.47	18.54
19	17.34	18.41
26	17.21	18.29
Nov 2	17.09	18.18

	Begins	Ends
9	16.59	18.08
16	16.50	18.00
23	16.43	17.54
30	16.38	17.50
Dec 7	16.35	17.49
14	16.35	17.49
21	16.37	17.51
28	16.42	17.56
Jan 4	16.48	18.02
11	16.57	18.10
18	17.07	18.19
25	17.17	18.28
Feb 1	17.29	18.38
8	17.40	18.49
15	17.52	19.00
22	18.03	19.10
Mar 1	18.14	19.21
8	18.25	19.32
15	18.36	19.43
22	18.47	19.54
29	18.57	20.05
Apr 5	20.08	21.16
12	20.18	21.27

	Begins	Ends
19	20.28	21.39
26	20.39	21.51
May 3	20.49	22.03
10	20.59	22.15
17	21.08	22.27
24	21.17	22.38
31	21.25	22.47
Jun 7	21.31	22.55
14	21.36	23.01
21	21.38	23.04
28	21.38	23.04
Jul 5	21.36	23.00
12	21.32	22.55
19	21.26	22.46
26	21.18	22.36
Aug 2	21.08	22.24
9	20.57	22.11
16	20.45	21.57
23	20.32	21.42
30	20.18	21.27
Sep 6	20.03	21.11
13	19.49	20.56

Rome

	Begins	Ends
Sep 28	18.37	19.38
Oct 5	17.25	18.26
1	17.13	18.15
19	17.02	18.04
26	16.52	17.54
Nov 2	16.43	17.46
9	16.35	17.38
16	16.28	17.33
23	16.23	17.28
30	16.20	17.26
Dec 7	16.19	17.25
14	16.20	17.26
21	16.22	17.29
28	16.26	17.33
Jan 4	16.32	17.38
11	16.39	17.45
18	16.47	17.52
25	16.56	18.00

	Begins	Ends
Feb 1	17.05	18.08
8	17.14	18.17
15	17.23	18.25
22	17.32	18.33
Mar 1	17.40	18.41
8	17.48	18.50
15	17.56	18.58
22	18.04	19.06
29	18.12	19.14
Apr 5	19.20	20.22
12	19.28	20.30
19	19.35	20.39
26	19.43	20.48
May 3	19.51	20.57
10	19.58	21.05
17	20.05	21.14
24	20.12	21.21
31	20.18	21.28
Jun 7	20.23	21.34
14	20.27	21.38
21	20.29	21.41
28	20.29	21.41
Jul 5	20.28	21.40
12	20.25	21.36
19	20.21	21.30
26	20.15	21.23
Aug 2	20.08	21.14
9	19.59	21.05
16	19.49	20.54
23	19.39	20.42
30	19.27	20.30
Sep 6	19.16	20.18
13	19.03	20.05

Zurich

Sep 28	18.52	19.57
Oct 5	17.38	18.43
12	17.24	18.29
19	17.11	18.17
26	16.59	18.05
Nov 2	16.47	17.55
9	16.38	17.46
16	16.29	17.38
23	16.23	17.33
30	16.18	17.29
Dec 7	16.16	17.27
14	16.16	17.28
21	16.18	17.30
28	16.23	17.35
Jan 4	16.29	17.41
11	16.37	17.48
18	16.47	17.57
25	16.57	18.06
Feb 1	17.08	18.16
8	17.19	18.26
15	17.29	18.36
22	17.40	18.46
Mar 1	17.51	18.56
8	18.01	19.07
15	18.11	19.17
22	18.21	19.27
29	18.31	19.37
Apr 5	19.41	20.48
12	19.51	20.59
19	20.01	21.10

	Begins	Ends
26	20.10	21.21
May 3	20.20	21.32
10	20.29	21.43
17	20.38	21.54
24	20.47	22.04
31	20.54	22.13
Jun 7	21.00	22.21
14	21.04	22.26
21	21.07	22.29
28	21.07	22.29
Jul 5	21.05	22.26

	Begins	Ends
12	21.01	22.21
19	20.56	22.13
26	20.48	22.04
Aug 2	20.39	21.52
9	20.28	21.40
16	20.17	21.27
23	20.04	21.13
30	19.51	20.58
Sept 6	19.37	20.43
13	19.23	20.29

ISRAELI FOLK DANCING

London

Hillel House—1-2 Endsleigh Street (near Euston Station)
Thursdays: 7.00p.m.–8.00p.m. (beginners)
8.30p.m.–11.00p.m. (advanced)
Call Maurice Stone at #388-0801

Paris

Centre Communitaire—18 boulevard Poissoniere
(Metro #8 or #9—rue Montmartre)
Wednesdays: 7.30p.m (no sessions in August)
Call Benny Assouline at #832-1909

Oslo

Jewish Community Center—Bergtein 13
Thursdays (every second Thursday): 7.30p.m.
Call Thor Henriksen at #N-2-23-58-21

Stockholm

Jewish Community Centre—Nybrogatan 19
Sundays: 4.00p.m.—9.00p.m. (no sessions in summer)
Call Zvi Wirchubsky at #31-81-08

Lyon

Call Yossi Choukroun at #893-5204

Strasbourg

Call D. Cudkovicz at #(88) 350-569

Rome

Call David Gerbi at #580-7691

Zürich

Call Sidney Weil at #(01) 202-66-84

Manchester

Habonim Bayit - 11 Upper Park (Salford 7)
Thursdays: 8.00 p.m.
Call David Bernstein at #(061) 428-7678

Bibliography

Aguilar,M. & Robertson,I. *Jewish Spain—A Guide* Altalena Editores, Madrid, 1984

Altshuler,D. *The Precious Legacy* Summit Books, New York, 1983

Barnett,R.D. & Levy,A. *The Bevis Marks Synagogue* University Press, Oxford, 1975

Bocher,O. *Der Alter Judenfriedhof zu Worms* Rheinische Kunststatten, Neuss, 1984

Cohen,S.R. *Scandinavia's Jewish Communities* The American-Scandinavian Review, Summer,1968

de Breffny,B. *The Synagogue* Macmillan Publishing Co. Inc., New York, 1978

Diamond,A.S. *The Building of a Synagogue—A Brief History* West London Synagogue, London

Encyclopedia Judaica Keter Publishing Company, Jerusalem, 1972

Flender,H. *Rescue in Denmark* Simon and Schuster, New York, 1963

Frank,B.G. *France for the Jewish Traveller* Air France, French Government Tourist Office, French Press and Information Services, French National Railroads, 1982

Gans,M.H.M.*History of Dutch Jewry from the Renaissance to 1940* Bosch & Keuning, Baarn, Netherlands, 1977

Grand,S. & Grand,T. *Exploring the Jewish Heritage in Spain* Spanish National Tourist Office, Spain, 1980

Jewish Rome Cultural Movement of Jewish Students, Mr. Emanuele Pacifici, the Jewish Community of Rome, the Rabbinical Office of Rome, the Centre for Jewish Culture, Rabbi Prof. Toaff, Prof. Saban, Mr. Armando Tagliacozzo, 1983

Kahn,L. *Geschichte der Synagogen in Basel* Israelitische Gemeinde Basel, 1968

Levenson,G. *Jewish Life in Scandinavia* SAS Scandinavian Airlines, United States, 1973

Levi,L. *Jewish Chronmony* Ministry of Religious Affairs, Jerusalem, 1983

Lightman,S. *The Jewish Travel Guide 1985* Jewish Chronicle, London, 1985

Maier,M. *The Jewish Cemetery of Worms* Worms, 1984

Mendleson,C. *The Jewish Museum Guide* Woburn House, London

Postal,B. & Abramson,S.H. *Traveller's Guide to Jewish Landmarks of Europe* Fleet Press Corporation, New York,1979

Servi,S. *The Synagogue of Florence* Florence Jewish Community, Florence, 1982

Stone,M. *Israeli Folk Dance Quarterly* Vol.2 Issue 2 London, 1982

Storti,E. *Jews and Synagogues of Venice, Florence, Rome, and Leghorn* Venice, 1973

Wagner,M. *Guide to Kosher Hotels and Restaurants in Europe* Swissair, Switzerland, 1983

Wigoder,G. *Jewish Art and Civilization* Chartwell Books, Inc., New Jersey, 1972

Wischnitzer,R. *The Architecture of European Synagogues* The Jewish Publication Society of America, Philadelphia, 1963

Vega,L.A. *The Beth Haim of Ouderkerk aan de Amstel* Van Gorcum & Co.,B.V., Assen, Netherlands, 1979

Yahil,L. *The Rescue of Danish Jewry* Jewish Publication Society, Philadelphia, 1969

Glossary

Ashkenazic Pertaining to Jews who lived in the Rhineland and spread through central Europe; the term eventually was used to include all Jews who observe the "German" synagogue ritual. The common language spoken by Ashkenazic Jews is Yiddish.

bimah The platform from which the Torah is read to the congregation during prayer services in the synagogue.

chassid A member of a Jewish mystical sect founded in Eastern Europe in the 18th century.

etrog (esrog) Citron used with a lulav at prayer services during the Festival of Tabernacles (Succoth).

Juderia A section of a Spanish town inhabited by Jews.

kiddush Special prayer recited over wine before the Sabbath or Festival meal.

kosher (kashruth) Ritually fit for use.

Ladino Dialect of Castilian, used as an everyday language by Sephardic Jews. Ladino is to Sephardic Jews as Yiddish is to Ashkenazic Jews.

lulav Palm branch used with an etrog at prayer services during the Festival of Tabernacles (Succoth).

Magen David Star of David.

Marrano Secret Jew, who lived in Spain during the Inquisition, who publicly observed Catholicism, but privately observed Judaism.

matzoh Unleavened bread eaten during the Festival of Passover.

mikveh Ritual bath; an important part of life for Orthodox Jewish women, who must immerse therein as part of the preparation for marriage, and who are required to cleanse themselves in it each month after the menstrual period.

minyan According to the Orthodox tradition, ten males over the age of thirteen, the minimum attendance required for congregational worship.

Rosh Hashanah Jewish New Year.

Sephardic Pertaining to the occidental branch of European Jews settling in Spain, Portugal, and parts of France and Italy.

shofar Ram's horn used during High Holy Day services.

shul Yiddish term for synagogue.

shulchan Special table used in the Holy Temple of Jerusalem.

shteebl Yiddish term for small room used for prayer services.

shtetl Yiddish term for small village or town.

succah A temporary booth or shelter used during the Festival of Tabernacles (Succoth), commemorating the journey of Israel through the desert after the exodus from Egypt. As their ancestors dwelt in temporary booths or shelters, so do contemporary Jews live in the succah during this week-long Festival.

yeshiva Hebrew (day) school.

Yiddish A High German language spoken by Jews in Eastern Europe and areas to which Jews from Eastern Europe have migrated. It is commonly written in Hebrew characters.

Yom Kippur Day of Atonement.

LECTURE PROGRAMS

by *Asher Israelowitz*

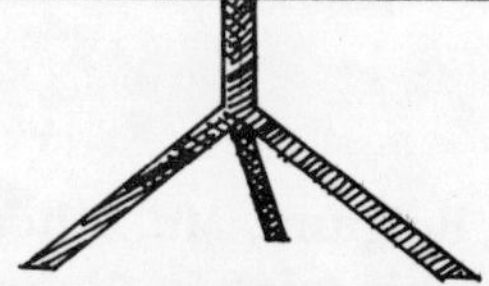

The Synagogues of Europe
The Wandering Jews of New York City
Jewish Landmarks of New York City
The Source of the Synagogue — Ancient Synagogues of Israel
The Synagogues of the United States — The Northeast

The multi-media programs (lecture, slide presentation, and sound track) are available for your special organizational meetings. For further information please write to:

Lectures
c/o Mr. Israelowitz
P.O. Box 228
Brooklyn, New York 11229

BIOGRAPHY

Born in Brussels, Belgium, Mr. Asher Israelowitz brings a rich background to his mission of documenting Jewish Europe. Besides his rabbinical training, he is also a professional architect and photographer. Among his noted architectural projects are the Synagogue and Holocaust Center of the Bobover Chassidim in Borough Park and the Yeshiva Chaim Berlin (elementary school) in Brooklyn, New York. He has exhibited his photographs at museums throughout the New York area, including the Brooklyn and Whitney Museums. The photographs in this guide are his own creations. His other books, *Synagogues of New York City* (1982) and *Guide to Jewish New York City* (1983), have been distributed worldwide and have received rave reviews. Mr.Israelowitz has appeared on several television and radio programs including NBC's *First Estate—Religion In Review*. In his spare time, Mr. Israelowitz gives lectures on various Jewish topics and also conducts guided tours.

Index

Aaron the Jew *178, 181*
Abarbanel, Issac *1*
Abulafia, Samuel Levi *13*
Ahvenanmaa Islands *173*
Algeciras *24*
Alhambra *5*
Alsatian Museum *43*
Altneuschul *134*
Altschul *136*
American Express Offices *19, 26, 29, 57, 89, 113, 124, 128, 139, 143, 147, 159, 161, 166, 170, 174, 176, 206*
Amsterdam *150*
Anne Frank House *155*
Ansbach *94*
Antonelli, Allessandro *84*
Antwerp *144*
Arch of Titus *61, 64*
Austria *127*
Avignon *44*
Avila *16*
Baldachino *67, 84*
Bamberg *103*
Barcelona *3*
Bar Giora, Shimon *64*
Basel *116, 120*
Beauberg Center *38*
Bechofen *96, 103*
Beit Hatefutsot *104*
Bejar *16*
Belgium *144*
Ben Israel, Rabbi Menasseh *156, 180*
Benjamin of Tudela *1, 67*
Bergson, Henri *33*
Berlin *96, 99*
Berlin Jewish Cemetery *98*
Bern *116, 120*
Bernini *67, 84*
Besalu *16*
Bevis Marks Synagogue *153, 184*
Black Plague *31, 109, 116*
Blatas, A. *77*
Bloch, Sir Maurice *195*
Blum, Leon *33*
Bohemia *134*
Bonheur *33*
Brussels *144*
Brustolon, Andrea *74*
Budapest *140*
Busito *86*
Cacarer *16*
Calahorra *16*
Cannes *48*
Canton Scuola *75*
Cardozo, Aaron Nunez *22*
Carmagnola *85*
Carmona *16*
Carpentras *44, 45*
Cassin, Rene *33*
Cavaillon *44, 46*
Ceasar, Julius *63*
Central Synagogue *140*
Chagall, Marc *33, 38, 48*
Chamonix *44*
Charles Bridge *136*
Chieri *84*
Chmielnicki *136*
Chuetas *8*
Ciudad Real *16*

Clifford's Tower *195*
Cluny Museum *40*
Cochin *149*
Cohen, Denis Bonchy *195*
Cologne *92, 99*
Colosseum *64*
Columbus, Christopher *6, 11*
Concentration Camp *100*
Conegliano *86*
Copenhagen *162, 164*
Cordoba *4*
Corregio *86*
Costa del Sol *7, 8*
Crimean War *173*
Cromwell, Oliver *156, 178*
Crusades *31*
Curacao *149, 153*
Czechoslovakia *130*
Dachau Concentration Camp *100*
David, Statue of *78*
Danish West Indies *162*
Dayan, Moshe *38*
De Leon, Moises
De Modena, Leone *63, 69, 74*
Denmark *162*
Diamond Bourse *144*
Dohany utca Synagogue *140*
Dublin
Duke's Place Synagogue *183, 193*
Dutch West Indies *149*
East Berlin *96*
East End of London *183*
Elche *16*
El Greco Museum *13–15*
Elsinore *164*
El Transito Synagogue *13*
Endingen *116, 118*
England *178*
Essen *102*
Estella *16*
Faro *28*
Fasanenstrasse Synagogue *99*
Ferdinand & Isabella *3, 6*
Finland *172*
Florence *78*
Follies Bergeres *40*
France *31*
Franco, Francisco *3*
Frank, Anne *155*
Frankfurt-am-Main *102*
Freud, Sigmund *134*
Gans, David *133, 137*
Garnethill Synagogue *195*
Germany *92*
Gerona *16*
Ghetto *64, 69, 70*
Gibraltar *22, 153*
Giudecca *69*
Glasgow *195*
Goldsmid, Sir Issac Lyon *180, 193*
Golem *135*
Gothenburg *168*
Granada *5*
Great Britain *178*
Great Portuguese Synagogue *150*
Guadalajara *16*
Halevi, Judah *1, 4, 11*
Hall of the Ambassadors *6*
Hamburg *111, 162*
Hamlet *164*
Haskalah *94*
Hassan, Sir Joshua A. *22*
Heller, Rabbi Yom Tov Lipmann *133*
Helsinki *172, 173*
Herzl, Dr.Theodor *120, 140*
Hervas *16*
Holland *149*
Holocaust Memorial *77*
Horb *104*
Hungary *140*
Ibn Ezra, Abraham *11*
Ibn Gabirol, Solomon *7*
Ibn Naghdela, Joseph *5*
L'Isle-sur-Sorgue *44*
Inquisition *1, 6, 14, 72, 152, 178*
Ireland *210*
Israel Museum *86, 104*
Israel Square *165*
Israeli Folk Dancing *40, 210*
Israels, Joseph *155*
Italy *61*
Judah Loew, Rabbi *133, 135, 137*
Jewish Art Museum of Paris *38*
Jewish Historical Museum of Amsterdam *154*
Jewish Museum of London *191*
Jewish Museum of Rome *67*
Jewish Theological Seminary *142*

Jewish Town Hall *138*
Jews' Bridge *66*
Jews' Island *119*
Kafka, Franz *134*
Kahan, Claude *33*
Karo, Rabbi Avigdor *133, 137*
Kilts *195*
Kishinev Pogroms *162*
Klaus Synagogue *137*
Kosher Restaurants *19, 26, 29, 55, 88, 113, 123, 128, 143, 146, 159, 170, 173, 177, 204, 210*
Kristallnacht *95*
Kusari *12*
Leghorn *81*
Lengnau *116, 118*
Levantine Scuola *73*
Lincoln Cathedral *178, 181*
Lisbon *27*
Liszt, Franz *140*
Livorno *81*
London *183*
Longhena, Baldassare *72*
Louvre *38*
Lower East Side *34, 180, 186*
Lucena *16*
Lunéville *41*
Luxembourg *161*
Lyon *44*
Madrid *6*
Maharal *133, 135, 137*
Maharam *12, 107*
Maharil *109*
Mahler, Gustav *134*
Maimanides, Moses *1, 4, 5*
Mainz *92*
Maisel, Marcus Mordecai *133, 137*
Majorca *8*
Malaga *7*
Mallorca *8*
Malmö *169*
Mamartine Prison *64*
Manchester *194*
Mantua *86*
Marbella *8*
Marble Arch Synagogue *193*
Marrano *1, 6, 11, 27, 72, 149, 152, 178*
Marseille *47*
McEwen, Sir John
Medicanelli *16*
De Medici, Cosimo I *81*
Meir of Rothenburg, Rabbi *12, 107*
Memorial of the Unknown Jewish Martyr *34*
Memorial to the Deported *35*
Mendes-France, Pierre *33*
Mendoza, Daniel *192*
Meyer, Rene *33*
Michelangelo *68, 78*
Mikvehs *19, 54, 87, 112, 122, 128, 142, 146, 158, 166, 170, 203*
Milan, Gabriel *162*
Milhaud, Darius *33*
De Modena, Leon *63, 69, 74*
Modigliani *33, 38*
Molcho, Solomon *137*
Mole Antonelliana *82*
Monaco-Monte Carlo *48*
Mondrian, Piet *157*
Mont Blanc *44*
Montefiore, Sir Moses *73, 81, 180, 193*
Montjuich *4*
Montmartre, rue de *40*
Monzion *16*
Moses, Statue of *68*
Munich *111*
Musafia, Benjamin *162*
Museum of the Danish Resistance *165*
Museum of the Diaspora *104*
Museum of Jewish Art *77*
Napoleon *33, 69, 149, 164*
Netherlands *149*
New Amsterdam *149, 153*
New York City *34, 149, 153, 180, 186*
Nice *47*
Nicolaievsky *172*
Norway *175*
Offenbach, Jacques *33*
Ogre Fountain *116, 120*
Old Jewry *183*
Ona *16*
Oranienburgerstrasse Synagogue *96*
Oslo *175*
Ostia Antica *68*

Ouderkerk *152*
Padua *86*
Palma *8*
Paredes de Nava *16*
Paris *34*
Pascin *33*
Pesaro *81, 86*
Petticoat Lane *186*
Philadelphia *153*
Pieta *67*
Pinkas Synagogue *138*
Pisa *81*
Pissaro *33*
Pletzel *34*
Plum Street Temple *140*
Pompidou Centre *38*
Portico d'Ottavia *66*
Porto *28*
Portugal *27*
Portuguese Cemetery *156*
Portuguese Synagogue *150*
Prague *130, 194*
Prague State Jewish Museum *134*
Provence *33, 44*
Rabenu Gershom *31, 92, 104*
Railroad Timetables *21, 30, 59, 91, 115, 126, 129, 147, 160, 167, 171, 174, 209*
Rambam *1, 4, 5*
Rashi *31, 92, 104*
Recife *149*
Reconquista *1*
Reggio Emilia *86*
Rembrandt *155*
Retti, Leopold *95*
Rijksmuseum *155*
Riviera *47*
Rock of Gibraltar *22*
Rome *61, 63*
Rosh *12*
De Rossi, Solomon ben Azariah *63*
Rothschilds *33, 38, 40, 180*
Rothschild Synagogue *35*
Royal Danish Library *165*
Saarebourg *42*
Sabbath Candle-Lighting Timetables *176, 211*
Saint-Saëns, Camille *140*
Sanhedrin *33*
Santa Maria La Blanca *13*
Sassoon, Albert *180, 181*
Scandinavia *162*
Scheiber, Dr.Sandor *142*
Schwäbisch Hall *103*
Scotland *195*
Segovia *9*
Seville *10*
Sfarad *1*
Shakespeare *164*
Shmuel ha-Magid *5*
Shum *92*
Sicily *61*
Siguenza *16*
Sistine Chapel *67*
Soncino, Gershom *63*
Soutine *33, 38*
Spain *1*
Spanish Inquisition *1, 6, 14, 72, 152, 178*
Speyer *92*
Spinoza, Baruch *156*
St.Michael's Cave *26*
St.Peter's Basillica *67, 84*
Stamford Hill
Stockholm *169*
Strasbourg *42*
Sullam, Sara Copio *69*
Sussman, Eliezer *103*
Sweden *168*
Switzerland *116*
El Transito Synagogue *13*
Temple Victoire *35*
T.G.V. *44*
Titus *61, 64*
Toledo *11*
De Torquemada, Tomas *6*
Tomar *28*
Touro Synagogue *153*
Trondheim *175*
Tur *12*
Turin *82*
Uppsala *168*
Valencia *17*
Vatican *67*
Venice *69, 149*
Vic *17*
Vienna *127*
Viipuri *172*

Viking Jews *162*
Virgin Islands *162*
Visigoths *1*
Vittorio Venneto *86*
West Berlin *99*
Westerbork *150, 155, 156*
West London Synagogue *193*
Westminster Synagogue *194*
Willemstad *149, 153*
William the Conqueror *178*
Wise, Issac Mayer *134*
Woburn House *191*
Wolfson, Sir Issac *195*
Worms *92, 104*
Wright, Frank Lloyd *157*
Yom Tov of Joigny *195*
York *195*
Youth Hostels *20, 30, 58, 90, 114, 125, 129, 139, 143, 147, 159, 161, 167, 171, 174, 176, 208*
Zamora *17*
Zaragoza *17*